Best Sights to See at

Voyageurs National Park

By Rob Bignell

Atiswinic Press · Ojai, Calif.

BEST SIGHTS TO SEE AT VOYAGEURS NATIONAL PARK

A GUIDEBOOK IN THE BEST SIGHTS TO SEE SERIES

Copyright Rob Bignell, 2018

Atiswinic Press
Ojai, Calif. 93023
dayhikingtrails.wordpress.com

ISBN 978-1-948872-01-0

Cover design by Rob Bignell
Cover photo of Beaver Pond at Voyageurs National Park

Manufactured in the United States of America
First printing April 2018

For Kieran

Contents

Introduction

Imagine a place where you can traipse beside massive ice age lakes and across some of the oldest known rocks on the planet, where you can hike through green boreal forests during the day and stare at the northern lights dancing against a velvet black sky at night, where you can watch moose graze in ponds and bald eagles soar overhead while gray wolves howl in the distance. The place is real: It's called Voyageurs National Park.

As a water-based park, plenty of opportunities for canoeing, motorboating, kayaking, houseboating, sailboating or jumping aboard a tour boat await in Voyageurs. In winter, cross-country, snowshoeing, and ice roads – paths plowed atop the frozen lakes – provide a number of adventures. The plentiful number of campgrounds, fishing camps, and other historical resort sites ensure you'll find a place of solitude and quiet. And you'll also find several miles of hiking trails, each offering a unique experience.

But with the national park's incredible size of 370 square miles, how can you ensure that you see its greatest wonders when vacationing or driving through? That's what "Best Sights to See at Voyageurs National Park" answers. In this volume, we've listed the top 10 most popular sights and detail the top day hiking trails to best experience them.

Geography

Located on Minnesota's northcentral border with Canada, Voyageurs National Park is a fairly flat region with rolling hills.

Measuring 218,054 acres in size, the water-based park boasts more than 500 islands and 655 miles of shoreline. The park's southern and eastern side sits on the mainland, but the bulk of the park is on Kabetogama Peninsula, which can be accessed only by boat.

Water makes up the majority of the park. Rainy Lake forms the park's northern boundary. Kabetogama Lake, on the southwestern side of the park, separates the Minnesota mainland from the peninsula. Namakan Lake is on the park's northeast side. Sand Point Lake and smaller Crane Lake below it forms the southwestern boundary.

On land, the boreal forest stretching across Canada has taken root in the foot of topsoil that has settled over the bedrock since the ice age ended about 10,000 years ago. The forest largely consists of birch and aspen, spruce and pine.

Thanks to climate change, elk and other native boreal forest species have moved north with neotropical birds new arrivals to the area. Whitetail deer and bald eagles are common in the park.

Geology

Eons ago, the area that now makes up Voyageurs National Park sat near the southern edge of Canadian Shield – a gigantic dome of volcanic bedrock that birthed North America. In fact, the park is one of the few places where you can see and touch rocks older than 2.8 billion years, more than half of the planet's age.

This early rock appears in multiple places. The bedrock on the shore of Sand Point Lake's Brown Bay is about 2.7 billion years old. Other outcroppings of the ancient stone can be seen near Echo Bay.

During the Archean, mountains were building in what is

now the park as another tectonic plate slid under the Canadian Shield. It was similar to the Pacific plate sliding against the North American plate in modern day California, leading to the rising of the Coast Ranges there. The result at Voyageurs was the creation of the bedrock that makes up the current state south to the Minnesota River Valley.

This same process caused in volcanic islands to form off-shore. The lava basins along the ancient fault lines eventually became greenstone belts that held a variety of metals and minerals, such as gold, silver and copper. An attempt was made in the park to mine gold from this belt during the 1890s.

Eventually, erosion wore down the volcanic mountain ranges. What happened afterward until about 190,000 years ago is a mystery, though.

That's because repeated periods of glaciation during the intervening years scraped off the topsoil and rock layers, exposing the Canadian Shield and ancient mountain building that left behind granite, biotite, schist, migmatite and greenstone. The last ice age about 11,000 years ago also finished gouging out several depressions; as retreating glaciers melted, the water settled in those massive troughs, creating the park's major lakes.

History

The Ojibwe had been long settled in the area that is now Voyageurs National Park when Euro-Americans arrived there. In fact, the names of many of the park's lakes – Namakan, Kabetogama and Natasha, among them – come from the Ojibwe language. The Ojibwe mostly lived on the lakes' shores, spearfishing and harvesting wild rice, as well as trading by canoeing across the region.

French-Canadian canoemen, later known as the Voyageurs,

soon realized the dozens of interconnected lakes made it an ideal route of travel, as they could traverse 3000 miles of waterways between Lake Athabasca in northwest Canada to Montreal.

Many voyagers paddled their 26-foot-long canoes for up to 16 hours a day as they crossed these waterways; the long days were necessary to avoid winter, as a canoe trip from Grand Portage, Minn., to the subarctic Canadian interior could take between four to five months. When they needed to walk between lakes or bypass a particularly rough stretch of water, they'd portage, or hike to the next shoreline, carrying their canoe and usually a 90-pound pack of furs. They whiled away the time in their canoes by singing, which set a rhythm to paddle by; usually their songs were about cavaliers, fair ladies, gallant captains, springtime, rosebuds and nightingales.

Many of the voyageurs were colorful characters, and not just in their behavior. They often wore a bright blue capote with red cap and sash as well as leggings and deerskin moccasins. Some who became Nor'westers – eight-man crews who rowed canoes that could carry up to 3000-pounds and often stayed the winter – earned the privilege of wearing a plume.

In addition to trade, a search for a water route between the Atlantic and Pacific oceans sent a number of explorers in the area. Among them was Pierre Gauliter de Varennes who in 1731 arrived in what is now Grand Portage. Two years later, they established Fort St. Pierre on Rainy Lake.

Ojibwe often supplied fur posts and canoe brigades with everything from food and birchbark canoes to "soft gold" – pelts of beaver and other animals that were popular in Europe.

In 1787, the international boundary between the United States and Canada (which at time was part of Great Britain) was established here between Lake Superior and Lake of the

Woods. Fifty-six miles of that boundary sits in the park.

Euro-American settlers began to arrive in large numbers during the 1800s. In 1865, gold allegedly was found on Vermilion Lake just south of the park, and then in 1890s gold was discovered in quartz veins on Little American Island. On the island, Rainy Lake City sprung up, boasting a population of more than 200, but the boomtown soon went bust and became a ghost town by 1901. A giant metal winch left by miners still remains among the ruins.

During the early 1900s, loggers came to the area. More than 40 logging camps operated in what is now the park between 1907 and 1922, so there are few big, old growth trees here.

Tourism and recreation began when U.S. Hwy. 53 opened in 1922 and has been the economic mainstay of the region for well over a half-century. Voyageurs became a national park in 1975 though the idea had been around since 1891.

Park Layout

This vast park can be divided into four general areas, each of which offers a number of great hiking trails.

Located a few miles east of International Falls, Rainy Lake is the most popular area. From there, park visitors can explore Rainy Lake and its islands, Black Bay, and make their way to Kabetogama Peninsula.

To the southeast is the Kabetogama area, which sits on the south side of Kabetogama Lake. There visitors can see and even walk atop rock almost half the age of the Earth.

Further east is the Ash River area, where said river flows into Kabetogama Lake. Several hiking trails run through this region's boreal forest.

Much of the park consists of the fourth region, the Kabetogama Peninsula. No roads lead to the backcountry peninsula, and it is only accessible by boat.

Each of the areas, other than the peninsula, maintains a visitor center.

How to Get There

The remote northern Minnesota park can be reached via U.S. Hwy. 53, which runs north from Duluth and east from International Falls.

From the Minneapolis-St. Paul area, take Interstate 35 north and then, once in the Duluth area, Hwy. 53 northwest.

From Thunder Bay, Canada, follow Ontario Hwy. 11 west to Fort Frances and cross into the United States. In International Falls, the route becomes Hwy. 53 or Second Avenue.

From Winnipeg, Canada, drive Manitoba Hwy. 12 east to Middleboro and enter the United States, where the provincial route becomes Minnesota Hwy. 313. Then go east on Minn. Hwy. 11 to International Falls and Hwy. 53.

Hwy. 53 offers access points to each of the park's visitor centers:

• County Road 129 heads to the Ash River Visitor Center and resort area.

• County Road 122 runs north to the Kabetogama Lake Visitor Center.

• Minn. Hwy 11 goes east from International Falls to Rainy Lake Visitor Center.

When to Visit

The best months to day hike the national park are June through September. Depending on the year, May and October also can be pleasant.

As with the rest of Minnesota, summers are humid, especially July and August. Rain can occur during the afternoon even when the morning is sunny, so always check the weather forecast before heading out.

November through April usually is too cold for day hiking. Once snow falls, trails typically are used for cross-country skiing or snowshoeing. Early spring often means muddy trails thanks to snowmelt and rainfall.

With so much water in Voyageurs, during summer you definitely will need to don mosquito repellent before hitting the trail. Be sure to carry the repellent with you in case it sweats off. Also, this far north, autumn nights will be cool and require sweatshirts and jackets.

Regardless of when you visit Voyageurs, entrance is free. It is one of the few national parks that does not charge an entrance fee, though you may need to pay for amenities such as boat rides, tours and campsites.

Kids Activities

A trip to Voyageurs National Park can be an educational experience for kids – though they may be having too much fun to even notice that they're learning!

The park delivers a variety of great activities that children can participate in from spring through autumn. Among the many offerings:

• **Junior Ranger Kids** – Kids between the ages of 5-12 can become a Junior Ranger. They'll first need to complete a Junior Ranger booklet (free at any park visitor center) then they can receive a Junior Ranger badge and certificate. Three different booklets are offered based on age.

• **Discovery Packs** – Free backpacks with a Voyageur Field Guide, telescope, pH strips, journal, three-legged race Velcro straps, scavenger hunt cards, magnifying glass, rock samples, and more can be checked out (and returned) at any visitor center to help kids and families explore the park together. Kids who check back in their pack receive a free Discovery Pack patch. Binoculars also can be checked out.

• **Kids' Art Show** – Kids PreK-6 can create artwork that is displayed annually during April's National Park Week at the Rainy Lake Visitor Center. Check online for the yearly theme.

Maps

To properly prepare for any hike, you should examine maps before hitting the trail and bring them with you (See the bonus Day Hiking Primer for more.). No guidebook can reproduce a map as well as the aerial photographs or topographical maps that you can find online for free. To that end, a companion website to this book offers printable maps for each featured trail at *dayhiking trails.wordpress.com/trail-maps.*

Best Sights

Voyageurs National Park is so large that unless you spend years there, you won't see all it offers. So when you've only got a few days at best to visit the park, what are the absolute must-sees? Following are the park's 10 best sights and the day hiking trails for getting to them.

Kabetogama Lake Overlook Trail's vista

Border Lakes

Kabetogama Lake Overlook Trail

Day hikers can explore the shores of a massive ice age lake on the Kabetogama Lake Overlook Trail.

The hike includes the 0.4-mile round trip trail and a 0.1-mile walk from the visitor center to a dock on the lake. They mark a good introduction to the park and lake after traveling across the mostly flat Minnesota landscape.

Five massive lakes, all carved out and filled by glaciers during the last ice age, sit in the park – Kabetogama, the much larger Rainy Lake to the north and west, Namakan Lake to the east, and smaller Sand Point and Crane lakes in the southwest. Rainy, Namakan and Sand Point all help form the U.S.-Canada international border.

Kabetogama Lake and a peninsula bearing the same name sit at the heart of the national park and sport the most activities for visitors.

A parking lot for the trail sits off Mead Wood Road north of County Road 129/Ash River Trail. This is the third pullout on your left as driving to the Ash River Visitor Center.

This short walk through the forest is handicap accessible with a minor elevation gain of 59 feet. That's enough of a change, though, to offer a grand view of Kabetogama Lake looking west.

At 25,000 acres, Kabetogama Lake is large, sporting 200 islands. It reaches a maximum depth of 80 feet.

The lake formed some 10,000 years ago when glaciers during the last ice age pushed out loose rock in the region, forming long, roughly west-east troughs. As the glaciers receded, meltwater settled in the troughs. About two of every five square miles of the park is water rather than land.

Today, the first thing any visitor to Kabetogama Lake notices on a sunny day is its peaceful blueness. Untouched by industry, the lake boasts an average water clarity of nine feet.

Kabetogama is highly regarded among walleye fishermen. Though cold even in July, its water remains slightly warmer, shallower and more fertile than the neighboring lakes, making it an ideal home for walleye, as well as northern pike, crappie, perch, bass, sauger, and smallmouth bass, all of which grow faster here.

Besides attracting fisherman, this draws bald eagles, which frequently can be seen flying across the lake. At the overlook, they soar between a couple of islands and the verdant shoreline of the Kabetogama Peninsula across the water.

After the overlook, continue driving north on Mead Wood Road to the visitor center. A rustic cabin, the center includes displays about the Ash River area's history, wildlife and fauna. Upon taking it in, walk the road on the center's west side to the lake. This leads to a small dock and a rock outcropping on which you can sit and enjoy the lake's beauty. Be forewarned that sometimes the wind can be heavy across the water.

Other Voyageurs Borders Lake Trails

If you love lakes, Voyageurs National Park is a great destination. Each of park's other major lakes can be seen via a day hiking trail:

• **Oberholtzer Hiking Trail –** A spur off the trail leads to a bench overlooking Rainy Lake, the largest of Voyageurs' waterbodies at 355 square miles. The trail starts near the Rainy Lake Visitor Center.

• **Beast Lake Trail –** This is a great trail to experience 39.2 square-mile Namakan Lake. It begins at the lake's Mica Bay and goes inland on Kabetogama Peninsula to much smaller Beast Lake.

- **Little Trout Lake Portage** – No trail runs alongside 8.1 square-mile Sand Point Lake. A waterway can be canoed from Sand Point Lake's Grassy Bay to Little Trout Lake with this small portage.
- **Casareto Cabin visitor destination** – The Kettle Falls Cruise heads to 4.6 square-mile Crane Lake, making a stop at this historic site on its north shore. In addition to walking through the historic area, visitors can dine at a hotel there.

Boreal Forest

Blind Ash Bay Trail

Day hikers can explore Voyageurs' boreal forest via the Blind Ash Bay Trail.

The 2.9-mile round trip trail sits at the southern tip of North America's vast boreal forest. To reach the trail, take U.S. Hwy 53 north from Duluth or southeast from International Falls. Turn east onto County Road 129/Ash River Trail then go left/ north on Mead Wood Road. Park at the Kabetogama Lake Overlook near the Ash River Visitor Center.

Spruce, fir and aspen

A stem to the main trail leaves from the lot's west side. It runs about 0.1 miles through the boreal forest.

Boreal forests – which account for a quarter of the planet's remaining forests – largely consist of spruce, fir and aspen trees. Because they exist in a cold climate, the decomposing of pine needles and other dead plants on the forest floor is slowed considerably, allowing for the storage of carbon that if otherwise released would heat up the planet.

At the first trail intersection, go left/west onto the main trail. The trail winds through the forest atop a rocky ridge. After crossing a maintenance road, you're entirely in the wilderness.

Blind Ash Bay Trail

As traveling through Voyageurs, you'll likely spot basswood, maples, oaks, paper birch, and pines common to the Northern hardwood forests of the Upper Midwest and New England. The national park marks the transition zone between the two eco-systems.

This far north in Minnesota and given the boreal forest, the types of animals you're likely to see also shifts from the temperate woodlands. Bald eagle, beaver, black bear, gray wolf, loon, moose, and a variety of owls and warblers inhabit the park. Any one of the birds can be heard if not see on the Blind Ash Bay Trail. Look for tracks of the mammals.

Water views on loop

About a mile from the stem trail, you'll the reach the loop. Go right/northwest on it.

Kabetogama Lake soon appears between breaks in the trees to the northwest. The massive lake boasts a surface area of 62 square miles. The Kabetogama is just one of four large lakes in Voyageurs; in fact, 40 percent of the park is water.

As the trail loops south then east, most of the water views are of Blind Ash Bay.

After 0.7 miles, the loop rejoins the main trail. Retrace your steps back to the parking lot.

Other Voyageurs Boreal Forest Trails

Voyageurs National Park is a great destination for exploring boreal forests. A few major park trails cross though this spruce-, fir- and aspen-dominated woods. Those trails include:

• **Beaver Pond Overlook Trail** – The short hike runs 0.4-miles round trip to a former beaver pond. A parking lot for the trailhead sits off of Mead Wood Road (on the way to the Ash River Visitor Center) north of County Road 129/Ash River Trail.

• **Kab-Ash Trail** – The 28-miles trail runs between the terminus of County Road 672/Salmi Road and the end of County

Road 129/Ash River Trail. It also can access it via a stem trail off of Hwy. 129 east of Hwy. 53.

• **Gold Portage Trail** – The Kabetogama Peninsula is virtually all boreal forest. The Gold Portage Trail, which runs 0.25-miles one way alongside the rapids-portion of the waterway connecting Black Bay and Kabetogama Lake, is a good way for hikers to experience it via canoeing.

Aurora Borealis
Oberholtzer Trail
Hikers can witness vivid displays of the aurora borealis at Voyageurs National Park.

One great day path to see the northern lights, as the aurora borealis is more commonly known, is the Oberholtzer Hiking Trail. The 1.7-miles round trip trail can be enjoyed during the day for its woodlands, lake view, and marsh, but at night its proximity to the Rainy Lake Visitor Center also makes it ideal for seeing these dancing lights.

To reach the trail, from International Falls take Minn. Hwy. 11 east to the park. Turn right/south onto County Road 96, aka Park Road; when Hwy 96 turns south, continue straight/east on Ut-342. Park in the lot for the Rainy Lake Visitor Center Public Boat Access, trying to find a space as close to the entry road as possible.

Walk along the side of the road toward the parking lot's junction with Ut-342; after a low, flat outcrop of rock but before the junction, look for the trailhead on the left/west.

The trail initially crosses an open area, running 0.35 miles to the beginning of its eastern loop. This stretch marks a great spot to stop and view the aurora borealis.

The light show occurs when charged particles from the sun strike the Earth's magnetosphere, which deflects dangerous

Aurora borealis at Voyageurs National Park. Photo courtesy of Voyageurs NPS.

radiation and other magnetic waves from space. After being deflected, the striking particles flow around the Earth, as if water striking a stationary rock.

Sometimes the charged particles penetrate the magnetosphere, until smashing into nitrogen or oxygen atoms. Which one the particles hit and at what altitude this collision occurs determines the light show's color.

Red lights means the particles are hitting oxygen, above 150 miles in altitude. If the particles hit oxygen below that altitude, they will be green. Purple is common when the particles contact nitrogen more than 60 miles above the surface. Blue occurs when hitting nitrogen below that height. Because of this, the northern lights can appear a variety of colors.

The aurora borealis will appear more intense in Voyageurs than at almost any other national park other than those in Alaska. That's because the northern lights are more prevalent in middle to higher latitudes as approaching the pole. Sometimes at Voyageurs, it fills almost the entire sky.

The best time to see an aurora is during a solar storm on a clear night when there is little or no moonlight. An aurora forecast with maps is available online from the University of Alaska Fairbanks at *auroraforecast.gi.alaska.edu*.

If hiking the full trail during the day, go left/east onto it. Most of the rest of the way is wooded.

In 0.12 miles, you'll come to a spur; go left/east into it, which in 0.05 miles leads to a bench overlooking Rainy Lake. All of Voyageurs' lakes abound with walleye, northern pike and smallmouth bass, and during daylight you're certain to see fishermen on the waters.

Once taking in the view, head back on the spur; at the loop, continue left/west. In 0.1 miles, you'll reach the junction with the main trail; go left/west onto it.

After 0.16 miles, the trail crosses County Road 96. Then in 0.06 miles, it reaches the western loop; go left/west on it.

The loop circles to the north and in 0.11 miles comes to a bench. In 0.03 miles from there, you'll reach the end of loop; continue by retracing your steps back to the first loop.

Rather than going on the east loop again, stay left/northeast; in 0.04 miles, you'll come to the other junction for loop. Keep left/north back and head back to the parking lot.

Oberholtzer Hiking Trail also is used as a snowshoe trail in winter.

Ojibwe Heritage
Ethno-botanical Garden Trail

Day hikers can learn how Ojibwe Indians flourished in the Upper Midwest on a new Voyageurs National Park trail.

The looping 0.25-mile Ethno-botanical Garden Trail runs

Ethno-botanical Garden Trail

through an Ojibwe encampment and the plants the Indians re-
lied upon before European-Americans settled northern Minnesota. The trail was created just a few years ago, and though
short, is packed with a lot of experiences.

To reach the trailhead, from International Falls take Minn.
Hwy. 11 east. Turn onto County Road 96 and follow the signs
to the Rainy Lake Visitor Center. Park there.

The trail leaves from the center's south side. Rock cairns
mark the way through the garden.

During the early 1990s, equipment dredging the boat basin
brought non-native, invasive red canary grass into the area.
The grass quickly overran the field between the boat basin and
visitor center.

Then, during the early 2010s, volunteers from a variety of
organizations worked together to plant a one-acre garden with

native vegetation, almost all of which were vital to the Ojibwe culture for food, medicine, ceremonies, and raw materials. To accomplish this, native seeds were collected from across the park, nurtured in the park's greenhouse, then transplanted in the garden.

Among the plants you can see there include: serviceberry and pin cherry, both of which blossom in spring; sweet fern, wild rose, raspberries, blueberries and strawberries in summer; golden yellow birch, aspen, reddish brown oak, and red maples in autumn; and red osier dogwood shrubs that contrast with the green of pines, firs and cedars in winter.

Plant markers set throughout the garden list the plant's name in English and Ojibwe.

The plants weren't just important to the Ojibwe but to the local ecosystem. Bees, for example, can be seen pollinating blossoms such as the native milkweed, a plant that monarch butterflies depend upon for survival.

At the heart of the trail is an Ojibwe Indian camp. You can step into a lodge called a waaginogaan, in which young, flexible birch poles are tied together with basswood roots for a frame and then birch bark is layered in for siding. Outside the lodge is an open air fire ring. Such rings often were the sites of communal cooking, ceremonies, and social gatherings. Drying racks for fish, venison, herbs and hides are nearby.

The camp includes a central fire ring like the Ojibwe used for communal cooking, meals and ceremonies. Sometimes volunteers manning the site cook traditional bannock, or fry bread, over the fire. You usually can also see freshly picked herbs hung to dry and fish nets stretched for drying and repair.

Each park visitor can pick up to a gallon of berries per day in the garden. A Junior Ranger Garden Explorer Book also is available for kids. The trail can be snowshoed in winter.

Ellsworth Rock Gardens. Photo courtesy of Voyageurs NPS.

Ellsworth Rock Gardens

Ellsworth Rock Gardens Tour

Day hikers can walk through a whimsical man-made rock garden on a ranger-led tour.

The Ellsworth Rock Garden Tour is short but includes the bonus of a boat ride across beautiful Kabetogama Lake. To reach the rock garden, from U.S. Hwy 53 turn north onto County Road 122/Salmi/Gamma Road. When Hwy. 122 turns left/west, continue straight/north to the Kabetogama Lake Visitor Center. Once there, you can purchase tickets for the boat ride to the historic site. The boat leaves from a visitor center dock.

During the lake crossing, be sure to cast an eye to the shoreline and sky. Active bald eagle nests can be spotted in the tree canopies, and the majestic raptors often circle and dive at the water to catch fish.

The boat arrives on Kabetogama Peninsula at a dock near the rock garden. From there, a park ranger leads visitors through the historic sight.

The trail starts at a historic signpost, winds pass the wayside exhibit, cuts through the sculpture garden past the stone circle and pond, with a spur to a teepee, and ends at a meteorite.

During the 1940s, Chicago carpenter and artist Jack Ellsworth landscaped 62 terraced flowerbeds on rock outcroppings at the sight. He planted more than 13,000 lilies as well as a variety of other flowers. Each dry-stacked wall encircling a flowerbed was layered with crushed white quartz, so that it appears like frosting. Pathways, stepping stones and bridges connected the terraced layers. Then he added 204 abstract rock sculptures, made from native stone. In all, this took more than two decades to complete.

The sculptures range widely in their complexity. Some simply are a single rock of an odd shape or color. Others consist of larger rocks and boulders mortared together to form tables, gateways, monoliths, spires and figures.

After 1965, Ellsworth never returned to the peninsula. He died in 1974.

A Minnesota Historical Society survey done two years later found that some rock garden items missing and a few sculptures tipped. By the end of the decade, the forest had reclaimed the flowerbeds.

Though the National Park Service purchased the property in 1978, the sight largely remained in a growing state of disrepair for the next 18 years. Then the park service, under pressure from the local Kabetogama Lake community, restored the flowerbeds and began repairing sculptures and nearby buildings. The effort is ongoing.

Historic photo of Little American Island gold mine operation. Photo courtesy of National Register of Historic Places.

Historic Gold Mine

Little American Island Trail

Day hikers can explore the only authentic gold mine discovered in Minnesota.

The Little American Island Trail loops 0.25 miles in at Voyageurs National Park's Rainy Day area. In summer, a boat is needed to reach the trail on Little American Island, but you can hike, snowmobile or ski there in winter.

If you need to hitch a ride there, the Grand Tour, a ranger-led boat tour, heads to and from the island in a Rainy Lake bay three days a week on summer afternoons. Along the way, you can see active eagle nests and a commercial fishing camp. The tour does charge a fee.

From the dock on the island's north side, the trail heads about 100 feet inland. At the first junction, go right/west on the trail. This loops over an adit, a passage that leads into a mine, usually built for access or drainage.

In 1893 while prospecting on the island, George Davis discovered the gold in a six-foot wide vein of quartz. He crushed some of it, and an analysis found about 25 cents worth of gold in the sample.

With that news, the island's owner, Charles Moore, sold the land to some Duluth businessmen, and mining began in earnest. To support the operation, Rainy Lake City sprung up on the east side of Black Bay Narrows about a mile southeast of the island. At its height, the mining town boasted a population of a few hundred with 17 saloons (which sold whiskey at 15 cents a glass), a dry goods store, lumberyard, bank, furniture store, bank, hotels, bakery, brick factory, post office and even a school.

At the next trail junction, go right/south. This spur leads to another shaft and a pile of tailings. Most of the mine's tailings were used to construct nearby International Falls' main street, causing many to jokingly nickname it the "city whose streets are paved with gold."

Returning to the main trail, go right/east. You'll pass a large pulley wheel that was attached to a winch for hauling gold-bearing rock out of the mine. After that is another adit.

During the height of the rush in 1894-95, a 200-foot shaft the trail passes was dug with about $5600 of gold mined.

Magma pushed the gold up to the surface about 2.1 billion years ago when a fault line ran through the area. The fault was similar to today's San Andreas Fault, caused by two tectonic plates sliding past one another, as this region was near the southern edge of the Canadian Shield, the beginning of the North American continent we know today.

In the late 1890s, many other mines, both shafts and exploratory pits, across the "Rainy Lake Gold Fields" were dug, but no more gold was found. The boomtown soon went bust and became a ghost town by 1901.

At the next junction, turn right/east. In about 200 feet is an overlook of scenic Rainy Lake. Once you've taken in the view, return back to the junction except continue walking straight/ west. The trail at the intersection that follow heads back to the dock; turn right/north onto it.

2.7 Billion-Year-Old Rock

Echo Bay Trail

Day hikers can walk atop rock almost half the age of the Earth on the Echo Bay Hiking Trail.

The 2.2-mile trail consists of three stacked loops, the third or northernmost of which really is intended to be used only as a ski trail. Part of the route runs alongside Kabetogama Lake.

To reach the trailhead, from U.S. Hwy. 53, go north on County Road 122. Turn right/east onto Northern Lights Road/ County Road 332. A parking lot is on the road's north side.

The excitement begins even before you reach the trailhead, however. On Hwy. 122 about 2.3 miles north of Hwy. 53, pull over where there's an exposure of black rock cutting across light gray granite. The gray granite is 2.7 billion years old, part of the Canadian Shield that was the forebear of the North American continent and among some of the oldest exposed rock on Earth.

The black rock is about 2.1 billion years old. As the continent began to split apart, magma was able to rise through the cracks and fill as well overlay some of the adjoining area. The magma, which cooled and hardened into the black mafic rock at the exposure, filled an area stretching more than 50 miles north through International Falls into Ontario.

Back at the trailhead, go right/east from the parking lot. The trail curves north through a forest and in 0.4 miles comes to a

Echo Bay Trail

junction. Go right/north and continue alongside Kabetogama Lake. The lake formed when an ancient glacial flow sometime during the past 2 million years carved out the valley. At the end of the last ice age some 10,000 years ago, glacial meltwater settled in the valley.

The trail begins to climb as approaching the lake, and the aspen forest gives way to a rocky pine-covered ridgeline. The outcroppings here are about 2.692 to 2.695 million years old.

When these rocks were formed, they were at the southern edge of the Canadian Shield. As neighboring islands and small continents slammed into the shield, it expanded until becoming the continent we know today.

In 0.7 miles, the trail reaches the junction with the third loop. Go left/south away from the lake. Should you accidentally turn onto the top loop, it runs for 1 mile and reconnects with the next junction.

The underlying and exposed rock here largely is schist. It began to form when a mix of rock flowed down the shield's continental slope into a deep sea and settled in a clay mixture, forming a sandstone known as graywacke. The buried graywacke then was compressed and heated, transforming into a flaky rock known as schist.

The trail soon leaves the ridge and ascends into the lowlands. At 0.2 miles, the trail junctions with the other end of the third loop; go left/south here.

The schist bedrock joined the Canadian Shield (which much of the schist had eroded from) when an ancient island arc known as the Wawa subprovince pushed north, raised and compressed it, then merged with the proto-North American landmass.

In 0.1 miles, the trail arrives at the northern end of the first stacked loop. Go right/west. In just a few steps, a spur to the left/south leads to the top of a knoll, offering an overlook of a wetlands. Many years ago, beavers created this wetlands area by flooding a forest of ash trees via their dam building. At one time, the dead trees served as a great blue heron rookery.

From the overview, take the spur back to the main trail and turn left/west. In addition to the ancient rocks and the beaver pond turned heron rookery, the sounds and sights of warblers and woodpeckers are a highlight of the hike.

The trail eventually curls south then east around the wetlands, arriving back at your parking lot in 0.8 miles.

Northwoods Wildlife and Birds
Beaver Pond Overlook Trail

You can spot iconic Northwoods wildlife – or at least signs of it during an off day – on the Beaver Pond Overlook Trail.

The short hike runs 0.4-miles round trip. A parking lot for the trailhead sits off of Mead Wood Road (on the way to the Ash River Visitor Center) north of County Road 129/Ash River Trail.

Before heading to the overlook to search for wildlife, check out the outcrops of coarse pink to red granite along the trail's edge. Some of the pink feldspar crystals are as large as four inches across, an amazing sight.

From the trailhead, the path climbs uphill to a rocky terrace.

Among the wildlife you might spot are moose. The largest animal in the national park, it can stand up to 6 feet high at the shoulders and weigh a thousand pounds. Only a few of the park's moose reside off the Kabetogama Peninsula, and beaver ponds are a great place to catch them enjoying a drink. Northern Minnesota represents the southern edge of the moose's range in North America with about 40-50 in the park. The park's moose population recently has declined, in part due to the increased heat during summer months thanks to global warming.

Predation from gray wolves also has taken a toll on the

Beaver Pond Overlook Trail

stressed moose population. The territories of about 6-9 packs, each consisting of about a half-dozen wolves, cross into the park, mostly on the peninsula. In addition to moose, wolves feed on deer and beaver. Though mainly gray in color, their coats also can be a red hue or even pitch black. Adult wolves are about 5-6 feet long; females weigh 50-85 pounds with males slightly larger at 70-110 pounds. Though reclusive, sometimes they can be seen crossing the park entrance roads, or their tracks can be spotted in the mud.

Also keep an eye out for black bear prints. About 150 black bears reside in the park. Common across forested regions of North America, the black bear is the smallest of the continent's three bear species. Ranging from 4 to 7 feet long from nose to tail tip, males can weigh anywhere from 150-300 pounds with females just slightly smaller. Omnivores, they feed on berries, carrion, honey, insects, nuts, and small mammals; sometimes they'll hunt small deer and moose calves.

If you don't see any of these three animals, just pause and hold a hand to an ear. You're certain to pick up red squirrels chattering and scampering around, as well as many of the park's many bird species. Warblers abound on the trail, and near sunset owls usually can be heard.

When you reach a break in the forest canopy, look up. You may very well see a bald eagle. A year-round resident of the park, bald eagles enjoy the park's tall white pines that line the large, deep lakes chockful of fish. About 42 breeding pairs reside in the park. Adults stand up to 35 inches high and sport a wingspan of six to eight feet.

Sightings or at least hearing the unmistakable, tranquil call of the common loon is even more likely. Around 190 loons call the park home. Their black body sports a white checkered pattern, which allows them to blend well with a lake's sparkling water. Adults are about 30 inches long with a wingspan of 60 inches.

Less likely to be seen flying the skies along this trail is the double-crested cormorant. Though populous in the park, they mainly reside on Rainy Lake's rocky islands. Cormorants typically are a dark brown or black with iridescent highlights, but during breeding season their throat pouch turns a bright yellow, and along with teal-blue eyes, they can stand out from a distance.

At the trail's end is the overlook, which sits high over a pond created by beavers, a common creature in Voyageurs and one of the very reasons that the park's namesake came here. During the 1700s, French-Canadian traders exchanged European goods for beaver pelts that the local Ojibwe obtained by trapping. Due to overharvesting over the next two centuries, by

1900 the beaver almost disappeared from the area. The population has rebounded, though, and about 3000 beavers now reside in the park.

Beavers are no longer active at the pond seen from the overlook, but you still can observe how they re-engineer their environment by damming streams and small rivers. As the pond fills, they construct a lodge in which they raise their young. Beavers have created hundreds of ponds across Voyageurs.

Once you've taken in the view at the overlook, retrace your steps back to the parking lot.

If looking to extend your hike, consider picking up the nearby **Sullivan Bay Snowshoe Trail**. The trailhead is located just north of the turnoff for the Beaver Pond Overlook Trail.

At 1.2 miles round trip, the Sullivan Bay trail is mostly flat with one small hill toward its end. The trail heads to a picnic area with a scenic overlook from Sullivan Bay's north shore.

Usually a loon or two can be seen on the bay; their diving and resurfacing, as well as their calls, can make for quite a show. In autumn, black-eyed Susans bloom trailside.

Canoe Country
Gold Portage Trail

For many who visit Voyageurs, the real park is the Kabetogama Peninsula.

Never mind that the peninsula makes up the bulk of the park's land area. The peninsula truly is the backcountry, accessible only by boat, a wilderness where you can canoe all day past spruce and birch forests that you camp under at night, a land of untamed rivers where you can fish for walleye or northern pike and not worry a wit about another human being encroaching on your spot or disturbing your peace.

The peninsula also is an incredible place to hike. You're certain to spot white-tailed deer along the trail and bald eagles flying overhead, as hearing loons calling and wolves howling in the distance, all while traipsing across narrow, primitive trails, just like the voyageurs used centuries ago.

Many of the trails on the peninsula actually are portages and can be reached by canoeing or kayaking to a specific campsite. Such is the case with the Gold Portage Trail, which runs 0.25-miles one way alongside the rapids-portion of the waterway connecting Black Bay and Kabetogama Lake.

You can reach the trail via one of two visitor centers. From the northwest, you can set out at the Rainy Day Visitor Center and head across Black Bay. At the bay's southeast corner, enter the Ash River. From the southeast, you can leave from the Woodenfrog State Forest Campground near the Kabetogama Lake Visitor Center. Row northwest past the Chief Wooden Frog Islands and enter the Ash River in Kabetogama Lake's northwest corner.

The rapids sits on the river about half-way between Black Bay and Kabetogama Lake. The farther inland, the more the river narrows until reaching the rapids. The portage runs along the river's northeast shore and cuts through boreal forest.

In total, the Kabetogama Peninsula is 118 square miles, which is almost the size of the U.S. Virgin Islands. And while there are no roads, there are moose – about 40 of them in a 2014 survey.

Other Kabetogama Peninsula Trails

For many visitors to Voyageurs, the national park's heart is the Kabetogama Peninsula. No roads lead to the peninsula, so the only way to reach it is by boat or plane. Once on it, most visitors' time is spent canoeing, camping in the backcountry, or hiking primitive trails.

Three centuries ago, voyageurs – shown here in a historical re-enactment, plied the waters now making up the national park.

Indeed, many of the trails are portages or near campgrounds. Most are not day hikes.

Among the peninsula's many trails, listed roughly west to east and secondarily north to south, are:

• **Black Bay Beaver Pond Trail** – The 1.2-miles round trip trail sits on the westernmost tip of peninsula separating Black Bay from Rainy Lake. It can be snowshoed in winter.

• **Black Bay Ski Trails** – These five stacked loops, stretching from 1 to 5 miles in length, take you through northern pine country to a scenic and active beaver pond. They continue the Black Bay Beaver Pond Trail; in winter, each can be reached via the Rainy Lake Ice Road.

• **Locator Lake Trail** – This 2-mile one-way trail takes you up and down a variety of hills and through forests and wetlands. It connects the northwest side of Kabetogama Lake to Locator Lake.

• **Cranberry Creek Portage** – Actually an unnamed trail, it's a portage where Cranberry Creek narrows.

• **War Club-Quill Lakes Portage** – This route connects its namesake lakes. War Club Lake is west of Quill Lake.

• **Quill-Loiten Lakes Portage** – The portage runs between Quill and Loiten lakes; Quill is west of Loiten.

• **Shoepack Lakes Portage** – The trail connects Shoepack and Little Shoepack lakes; the former is northwest of the latter.

• **Cruiser Lake Trail** – The 9.5-miles one-way trail links several lakes – Jorgens, Quarter Line, Elk, Agnes, with spurs to Brown and Peary – boasts two accesses from southside at Lost Bay and an access on its north side at Anderson Bay on Rainy Lake. Two stacked loops run between and north of Elk and Agnes lakes. This trail crosses the peninsula up rocky cliffs and down into remote wetland areas. If you are hoping to spot some of the park's larger wildlife, this trail improves the odds of spotting a moose or hearing a wolf's howl.

• **Brown Lake Trail** – The portage runs from Browns Bay on Rainy Lake to Brown Lake in the peninsula's interior.

• **Peary Lake Portage** – The short trail links Finger Bay on Rainy Lake to Peary Lake.

• **Anderson Bay Overlook Trail** – The short 1.75-miles loop is accessible from Anderson Bay on Rainy Lake, just past the Kempton Channel, or the north end of Cruiser Lake Trail. The trail takes you up a rocky cliff to a spectacular view of Rainy Lake. It can be snowshoed in winter.

• **Beast Lake Trail** – The route runs from Mica Bay on Namakan Lake for 0.25 miles to the south side of Beast Lake and for 2.5 miles to the Cruiser Lake Trail southeast of Brown Lake. This trail heads along a ridgetop; a steep climb at the beginning and at the end awaits the adventurous.

• **Ryan Lake Portage** – The trail connects Rainy Lake to Ryan Lake on the peninsula's east side.

• **Hoist Bay visitor destination** – This 0.25-mile ranger-led tour of old logging camp and of a historic resort site sits on Namakan Lake's Hoist Bay east of the Ash River area. The Hoist Bay boat tour leaves from Kabetogama Lake Visitor Center for the site. During the boat ride, watch for active eagle nests.

• **Kettle Falls Historic District visitor destination** – The ranger-led Kettle Falls Cruise makes a two-hour stopover here. Hikers can traipse around the historic site and walk to an over-look of the neighboring dam, as well as dine at a hotel or enjoy a picnic lunch. The restaurant will prepare and serve any wall-eye you catch while fishing on the site. You also can play a nick-elodeon and toss horseshoes on the front lawn. The site is on the Canadian border in the park's northeast corner.

• **Casareto Cabin visitor destination** – The ranger-led Kettle Falls Cruise also spends two hours here, where you can traipse the historic site and dine at a hotel. The site is on the north side of Crane Lake in the park's southeast corner.

• **Little Trout Lake Portage** – This short portage connects Grassy Bay on Sand Point Lake to Little Trout Lake.

Wetlands

Rainy Lake Recreation Trail/International Falls Bike Trail

Visitors to Voyageurs National Park looking for an easy trail to hike or bike will enjoy the new Rainy Lake Recreation Trail.

Opened in 2015, the fairly flat, paved trail covers 1.7 miles one-way in the park's Rainy Lake area. If looking for a longer walk or bicycle ride, the trail conveniently connects to the International Falls Bike Trail, which runs for another 12 miles.

To reach the trailhead, from International Falls take Minn.

Hwy. 11 east. Turn on County Road 96 and follow the signs to the Rainy Lake Visitor Center. Park at the center.

Before heading out onto the trail, stop at the center to enjoy its exhibits, children's activity center, and small theater for a film about the park. Rainy Lake is the only one of the park's three visitor centers that operates year around. A bike rack, picnic table, and benches are available at the visitor center plaza.

From the visitor center, the trail runs alongside the park road and County Road 96, dipping into the woods and curling around rock outcroppings.

Anytime there are lakes and rivers flowing into them, the landscape will feature bordering wetlands. Voyageurs National Park is no exception, and the Rainy Lake Recreation Trail/International Falls Bike Trail, when it nears Rainy Lake or a tributary's shoreline, passes plenty of them.

The wetlands seen today along the trail today likely will look different in a few years. The park is working hard to rid the wetlands of invasive hybrid cattails and replace them with such natives as bur-reed, bulrushes and wild rice.

Exactly how to best do that is a question mark for the moment. Removing by hand, fire and mechanical harvesters all are being tested, and in varying settings one method may be better than the other.

The hybrid cattails so common in Voyageurs' many wetlands arose when native broad-leaved cattails crossed with narrow-leaved cattails brought here from Europe. The hybrid grew faster and in denser stands than native species.

That proved a disaster for native fish and waterfowl relying on native plants. The dense stands decreased spawning habitats for black crappie, golden shiners, northern pike and white suckers. As the hybrid filled in ponds, they left little forage and

Rainy Lake Recreation Trail/International Falls Bike Trail

few resting spots for migrating waterfowl and songbirds, re-ducing their populations.

The trail reaches the International Falls Bike Trail at the

junction of County Road 96 and Hwy. 11. Running 12 miles, the bike trail offers views of Rainy Lake, heads through woodlands, and passes marshes and lakefront neighborhoods. A portion of the bike trail is in Koochiching State Forest.

At Jackfish Bay, the Bike Trail becomes a designated on-road shoulder route, which is fine for bicyclists but not so great for hikers or walkers. It turns back to an off-road trail after heading through Ranier.

After passing the Voyageurs National Park Headquarters in International Falls and running alongside Rainy Lake's southern shore, the trail ends downtown. Parking is available in the Chamber CVB lot (301 2nd Ave.), close to where U.S. Hwy. 53 meets Minn. Hwys. 11/71. The trail is a quarter mile east of the CVB office.

Wheelchair accessible, the connected trails are open to walkers, bicyclists, runners and snowshoers. Pets are allowed but in the national park must be on a lease of no more than 6 feet and attended to at all times.

Nearby Trails

Several million acres of forest and public land surround Voyageurs National Park. Each boasts a number of great trails that pass fascinating rock formations, head to little seen waterfalls, and offer inspiring vistas at along the way. Most of these trails can be found in one of three regions: the **International Falls area**, east of the city as heading through Koochiching State Forest to the national park's Rainy Lake Visitor Center; **Kabetogama State Forest**, which sits south of the park's Kabetogama and Ash River visitor centers; and **Superior National Forest**, which includes the Boundary Waters Canoe Area to the park's west.

Tilson Bay Trail

International Falls Area

Tilson Bay Trail

Casual visitors to Voyageurs National Park often worry about hiking deep into the backcountry, where getting lost among black bears and gray wolves always is a possibility. One solution that allows you to enjoy the region's scenery without straying far from civilization is the Tilson Bay Trail, located just outside of the park's Rainy Lake area.

The 1.6-mile round trip trail consists of a side trail and a loop at one end. It's near a major highway and surrounded by a housing development but is nestled far enough away from both to give you that back-to-nature feel, especially as part of it is in the Koochiching State Forest.

To reach the trail, from International Falls, take Minn. Hwy. 11 east. Immediately after crossing Tilson Creek, turn left/ south into parking lot. Walk to the other side of the highway into the boat launch area for the trailhead.

The trail quickly climbs, crossing rock outcroppings to an overlook of the surrounding forest.

At the first junction, go left/northeast onto a side trail. You're now officially in the state forest. At 567,985 acres in size, the state forest crosses three counties.

You're certain to find a variety of trailside wildflowers. In spring, the white blossoms of wild strawberry and blueberry flowers as well as violets are common, and the bright green glow of new aspen leaves are particularly impressive.

The next junction rejoins the main trail. Go left/east onto it. You'll then cross a few small boardwalks that'll keep your feet dry in wet areas.

After that, the trail crosses County Road 137 and parallels that road, passing a Little Free library along the way, and re-enters the woods. The trail then splits to form a loop. Which way you go on the loop doesn't much matter; from either direction, the woods opens up to a view of Tilson Bay on Rainy Lake.

Upon completing the loop, retrace your steps back to the junction for the side trail. Rather than go on the side trail, though, continue left/straight west. You'll soon pass the first junction for the side trail.

The trail again climbs past the first set of rock outcroppings you went over then descends to the parking lot.

The trees, flowers and rock formations along the trail resemble much of the rest of Voyageurs National Park's Rainy Lake area. An entry to the national park is just a mile to the east.

Tilson Connector Ski Trail and Tilson Creek Ski Trails

The Rainy Lake section of Voyageurs National Park nicely connects with several trails in neighboring Koochiching State Forest.

Tilson Connector Ski Trail

The 0.93 mile one-way trail links the national park's Rainy Lake Visitor Center to the Tilson Creek Ski Trails.

To reach the trailhead, park at visitor center and head west from the lot, paralleling the park road. When the trail splits, go left/southwest, crossing County Road 96.

The trail passes through a wetlands then through a wooded area.

Also known as Voyageurs Tilson Trail, once in the state forest it becomes the Blue Trail of the Tilson Creek Ski Trails.

Tilson Creek Ski Trails

The Tilson Creek Ski Trails consists of 10 miles of ski trails arranged in several stacked loops, delineated on state forest maps by color.

Several routes are possible, ranging from short loops to longer excursions. The Blue Trail consists of three stacked loops with the last one joining the Orange Trail. South of the Orange Trail are the Yellow and then the Red trails. North of the Orange is the Green Trail.

In summer, grass quickly overgrows on these trails, so this is a good hike for dry days in spring or autumn after a good frost has knocked down the foliage. During winter, hiking is not allowed on the ski trails.

You also can access the trail system via the Green Trail. To do so, use the parking lot on the south side of Minn. Hwy. 11 east of International Falls in the Koochiching State Forest; this is the same lot used for the Tilson Creek Trail on the highway's north side.

Kabetogama State Forest
Ash River Falls Trail

Day hikers can head to a three-story waterfall on the Ash River near Voyageurs National Park.

The Ash River Falls Trail runs 1.7-miles round trip. Though not an official trail in the Kabetogama State Forest, the falls is so spectacular a sight that people have cut a path to it.

To reach the trail, from U.S. Hwy. 53 about midway between Ash Lake and Ray, turn east onto County Road 129/Ash River Trail. Then go right/south onto Ash River Recreational Trail. The paved highway naturally becomes Bright Star Road. As taking the last curve before the NoVA Far Detector Building (which is off limits to the public), park in the pullout on the road's left/northwest side. Two trails start at the pullout. Take the one on the right and go northeast.

Aerial photo of Ash River Falls

The sandy jeep trail heads through a woods as it wraps around the detector building. A particle physics experiment designed to detect neutrinos, elementary particles are beamed through 503 miles of Earth from Fermilab (the near detector) to this one in northern Minnesota (the far detector).

After about 0.42 miles, on the detector building's east side, the trail narrows and heads through a pine barrens.

Where the woodline picks up abut 0.38 miles later, the trail descends through evergreens to the Ash River shoreline. Once on the rocky beach, turn right/south; the base of the waterfall is in about 300 feet.

The Ash River tumbles about 34.5 feet over four tiers of gray rock. You'll likely spot a canoeist or two on the river below the falls; this is a popular canoeing destination from a series of resorts along County Road 129, which begin about a mile upstream. Unfortunately, no hiking trail leads from the resorts to the falls.

Below the waterfall, the river widens significantly and flows northeast to Sullivan Bay, which empties into Kabetogama Lake near the Ash River Visitor Center in Voyageurs National Park.

Gheen Hills Trails

Hikers can spot wildlife and various songbirds on the easy to reach Gheen Hills Trails south of the national park near Orr.

The 4.5-mile system of trails is popular with mountain bicyclists and cross county skiers as well as hikers. Multiple trailheads access the system.

The system is best done in late spring or early summer. Parts of the trail during early to mid-spring can be soggy, and in late summer overgrown with grass, which sometimes hides logs that can be tripped over.

Deer and bear

One good route in the Gheen Hills to day hike is a short loop that covers the trail system's northeastern woods.

To reach the trailhead, from Orr travel south about 3.5 miles on U.S. Hwy. 53. Turn right/west onto Diamond Match Forest Road. A parking area and the trail is less than 200 feet from the intersection.

The trail heads southwest from the lot across open country. This stem to the loop runs about 0.1 miles.

Where the trail divides, go right/west onto the loop, which quickly enters a forest. The majority of trees are stands of aspen, birch and pine.

White-tailed deer and black bear are the largest mammals in the area. Very rarely, moose and wolf make their way into this section of the Kabetogama.

Three songbirds

You have a much better chance of spotting three particular songbirds. Least flycatchers, mourning warblers, and the Nashville warblers all make their home along the trail system. Both warblers are yellow-breasted with the mourning warbler

Gheen Hills Trails

nesting here.

Along the way, there are a few intersecting trails that take you deeper into the Gheen Hills. To stay on the loop, always make a left turn at a trail intersection.

When you exit the woods (You'll be heading roughly north-east.), you've reached the end of the loop, which runs about 0.4 miles. Go right/northeast onto the stem trail and return to the parking area.

In all, this segment is about 0.6 miles long.

Other Kabetogama State Forest Trails

If driving north from Duluth to Voyageurs National Park, you'll first have to pass through the expansive Kabetogama State Forest. Covering 967 square miles, fir, spruce, aspen, pine, maple, and birch cover the public lands.

Plenty of great trails and forest roads perfect for hiking ramble through those woodlands. With the state forest's entire northern boundary adjoining Voyageurs, a number of trails can be found near the national park. Most of these can be explored on a day hike.

They include:

• **Arrowhead State Trail segment** – The combination snowmobile/hiking trail runs 135 miles from south of International Falls to west of west of Tower. Park in the turnaround at the end of the road heading east off of County Road 122/ Gamma Road immediately north of U.S. Hwy. 53. Go east on the trail down a hill to a stream flowing into Kabetogama Lake for a 1.5-mile round trip.

• **Ash River Falls Trail segment** – Two sets of stacked loops make up the ski/hiking trail. Park at the western trail-head parking lot off of County Road 129 east of Hwy. 53 and hike the first stacked loop for a 1.8-mile trip.

• **Echo Lake Hunter Walking Trail** – The trail rambles 13 miles through a young aspen forest and is prime ruffed grouse habitat. For the trailhead, go 2.2 miles from the County Roads

24/116 junction northeast of Orr.

• **Orr Bog Walk** – This 0.5-mile loop consists of a floating boardwalk through six wetlands environments. Pick up the trailhead behind the Voyageur Country Visitor Center in Orr.

• **Orr Spur North Trail** – The 8-miles one-way snowmobile trail connects the northern end of Orr to the Arrowhead State Trail near the Pelican River. Park off of County Road 180 near the river and head south from the Arrowhead for the trail's quietest segment.

• **Orr Spur South Trail** – Also 8-miles one-way, the snowmobile trail heads from U.S. Hwy. 53 to the Arrowhead State Trail near Little Elbow Creek. The western end of the trail crosses the Pelican River.

• **Pelican Lake Trail segment** – The trail runs from Hwy. 53 in Ash Lake to the north shore of Pelican Lake. Park off the highway alongside County Road 519 and walk to the creek flowing into Ash Lake for a 2.5-mile round trip.

Superior National Forest
Vermilion Gorge Trail

Day hikers can explore a narrow river gorge just outside of Voyageurs National Park.

The Vermilion Gorge Trail runs 3-miles round trip in Minnesota's Superior National Forest. Sporting a 282-foot elevation gain over the Vermilion River, it's best done in April through October and on dry days to avoid slick rocks.

To reach the trailhead, from U.S. Hwy. 53 in Orr, head north on County Road 23 for about 15 miles. In Buyck, take County Road 24 north for about 10 miles; a ranger station is located near end of Hwy. 24. The trailhead is in the parking lot across from the businesses just north of Crane Lake Ranger Station.

The gravel trail initially gains elevation then descends on

timbered steps with boardwalks over wet areas. Birch and aspen tower overhead.

This area was well-known to early European explorers even as the interior of what is now Minnesota remained terra incognita. Rene Bourassa ran a fur trading post at the mouth of the river on Crane Lake during the 1730s.

What really attracted European-Americans to the location, though, were minerals. In 1865, first iron ore then gold were reported discovered on Vermilion Lake. The latter set off the famous Vermilion Lake Gold Rush, and by 1866, about 300 people were panning for gold on the lake. No gold was found, but deep iron ore deposits were confirmed. The mining and logging industries soon followed, but today tourism provides most locals with their livelihoods.

Once out of the low-lying area, the trail enters a red pine stand. Be aware that bears do inhabit the area; be noisy on the trail to warn the bears in the distance of your presence so that you don't startle one up close.

After 0.75 miles, the trail reaches the Vermilion River. You can take more steps to the shore and a bobbing dock that floats on the river to get a good view of it in this wide section.

Once you've taken in the river, continue to the dock's right and head up several large rocks. Moss covers many boulders, and bunchberry bushes dominate. The trail narrows and turns to dirt, as taking a sharp turn and following the river upstream.

The path climbs steeply over rocks and roots to an overlook at the gorge's side. The sheer granite cliff walls are steep, so be careful to not fall.

Between the cliff sides is a 500-foot long narrows through which the Vermilion River takes a perpendicular turn before flowing into Crane Lake.

At the overlook, look west to a marshy plain created by the

river spreading out. Sunsets are impressive here. Though not visible from the overlook, Vermilion Falls is a few miles upstream.

Upon reaching a large rock wall, the trail ends. Retrace your steps back to the parking lot.

Dogs are allowed on the trail but must be leashed.

Vermilion Falls Trail

Day hikers can enjoy one of the few waterfalls in or near Voyageurs National Park on the Vermilion Falls Trail.

The trail to the falls is an effortless walk. Fortunately, the sight makes for easy lingering given the long drive to the falls.

To reach the trailhead, from U.S. Hwy. 53 in Orr head north on County Road 23 for about 15 miles. In Buyck, take County Road 24 north then turn left onto Forest Road 491. Drive 5.45 miles. You're driving through the Superior National Forest and closing on the Vermilion Falls Recreation Area. Turn right/ south onto the road heading to the Vermilion Falls Overlook and park at the lot along the loop. If you've crossed the Vermilion River, you've driven too far.

From the lot, a short handicap accessible trail heads south over a wooden boardwalk to an observation deck of the falls. It is about 0.25 miles round trip.

The Vermilion River tumbles 25 feet over rapids and a large slope through a 10-foot wide gap in the rock.

Smallmouth bass abound in the river below the falls. Crappies, northern pike and walleyes also can be found in the river, which flows out of Lake Vermilion for 40 miles to Crane Lake.

After taking in the falls, head back to the lot. Before reaching it, however, do some of that lingering by turning left/west onto the rugged portage trail. Slightly shorter than the trail to the falls at 0.2-miles round trip, it takes hikers to a scenic view of

The Vermilion River roils 25 feet down rapids and a small drop.

the river above the falls.

Returning to the falls trail, continue straight/east onto the river trail. The route runs downstream from the falls.

In about 0.25 miles, the river trail meets Forest Road 491. Here on the opposite shore of the river is an extensive wild rice bed. Its shoots usually peak above the water around mid-July. Wild rice actually is an aquatic grass rather than a cereal grain; both people and local wildlife enjoy its seeds and harvest it in late August through October.

Cross the forest road and continue the trail north for about 0.1 miles to The Chute. This is a constriction in the river, forming a Class III-V rapids. Sometimes you pass canoeists on the trail using it as a portage around the rocks.

The trail ends just a little past the rapids; from there, retrace your steps back to the parking lot. In total, you'll have walked 1.45 miles between the falls, portage and river trails.

A small picnic area and toilets are available along the trail.

Other Superior National Forest Trails

• **Bug Creek Walking Trails** – The trail system heads through a forest of young aspen growing on just-logged lands to a small pond on Bug Creek in Superior National Forest. A trailhead can be found off of County Road 203 about 11 miles from Orr.

• **Herriman Lake Trail** – More than half of the 13 miles of trails in this system run through the Boundary Waters Canoe Area Wilderness. The trailhead is in Superior National Forest, off of County Road 24 about 27 miles northeast of Orr.

Boundary Waters Canoe Area Wilderness

Many visitors to Voyageurs National Park combine it with a trip to Minnesota's famous Boundary Waters Canoe Area Wilderness.

Though most people think of Boundary Waters as a great place to canoe or kayak – and it is – the region also is an excellent spot for primitive hiking. In addition, segments of a number of the area's long backcountry trails can be done as day hikes.

Located in northeastern Minnesota along the Canadian border, the BWCAW offers more than 150 miles of portage trails, 2000-plus campsites, and over 1000 portage-linked lakes. Exceeding a million acres in size, the BWAC holds the largest old-growth forest east of the Rockies. Technically part of Superior National Forest, National Geographic recently listed the BWCAW as one of "50 Destinations of a Lifetime."

The quickest way to reach the Boundary Waters from Voyageurs is through the city of Ely. To reach Ely, from Voyageurs take U.S. Hwy. 53 south. Turn left/east onto Minn. Hwy. 1, which heads into the city.

Among the many BCWCA trails easily accessible from Ely

are:

- **Big Moose Hiking Trail** – The 3-mile out-and-back trail (6-miles round trip) heads through a conifer forest to Big Moose Lake's northern shore; the last quarter mile of the trail is within the Boundary Waters Canoe Area Wilderness. Park in the lot along Forest Road 464, southwest of Echo Trail about 20 miles northwest of Ely.

- **Burntside Lake North Arm Trail** – A number of trails connect Burntside State Forest to the BWCAW and Chippewa National Forest, including this 2-mile loop from North Arm to Slim Lake. To reach the trailhead, take County Road 644 to the parking lot near the highway's end along the North Arm of Burntside Lake.

- **Kekekabic Trail segment** – Known as "The Kek," the trail runs 41 miles from north of Ely to Grand Marais; its western trailhead easily can be day hiked through an aspen, jack pine and conifer forest to the shores of Snowbank Lake and then back for a 4-mile round trip. The trailhead is off of Snowbank Lake Road in the BWACW, just under 20 miles east of Ely.

- **Secret/Blackstone Trail segment** – A 1.33-mile segment of this 8-mile trail can be done around scenic Blackstone Lake. The trailhead is about 20 miles northeast of Ely, off of Moose Lake Road (County Road 438) across the road from La Tourell's Resort.

- **Sioux Hustler Trail segment to Devil's Cascade** – For fit families with a lot of energy and a whole day to spend, this 11-mile round trip in the BWCAW rewards with the 75-feet Devil's Cascade through a granite gorge. Park at BCWAW Entry Point #15 off of Echo Trail northeast of Ely.

- **Snowbank Lake Trail** – The 25-mile trail around Snowbank Lake in the BCWAW can be shortened to a 2.5-mile out-and-back segment. Use the same trailhead as described above for the Kekekabic, except go north; take the first spur east to the Snowbank Lake's shore.

Bonus Section:
Day Hiking Primer

Y ou'll get more out of a day hike if you research it and plan ahead. It's not enough to just pull over to the side of the road and hit a trail that you've never been on and have no idea where it goes. In fact, doing so invites disaster.

Instead, you should preselect a trail (This book's trail descriptions can help you do that). You'll also want to ensure that you have the proper clothing, equipment, navigational tools, first-aid kit, food and water. Knowing the rules of the trail and potential dangers along the way also are helpful. In this special section, we'll look at each of these topics to ensure you're fully prepared.

Selecting a Trail

For your first few hikes, stick to short, well-known trails where you're likely to encounter others. Once you get a feel for hiking, your abilities, and your interests, expand to longer and more remote trails.

Always check to see what the weather will be like on the trail you plan to hike. While an adult might be able to withstand wind and a sprinkle here or there, for kids it can be pure misery. Dry, pleasantly warm days with limited wind always are best when hiking with children.

Don't choose a trail that is any longer than the least fit person in your group can hike. Adults in good shape can go 8-

12 miles a day; for kids, it's much less. There's no magical number.

When planning the hike, try to find a trail with a mid-point payoff – that is something you and definitely any children will find exciting about half-way through the hike. This will help keep up everyone's energy and enthusiasm during the journey.

If you have children in your hiking party, consider a couple of additional points when selecting a trail.

Until children enter their late teens, they need to stick to trails rather than going off-trail hiking, which is known as bushwhacking. Children too easily can get lost when off trail. They also can easily get scratched and cut up or stumble across poisonous plants and dangerous animals.

Generally, kids will prefer a circular route to one that requires hiking back the way you came. The return trip often feels anti-climatic, but you can overcome that by mentioning features that all of you might want to take a closer look at.

Once you select a trail, it's time to plan for your day hike. Doing so will save you a lot of grief – and potentially prevent an emergency. You are, after all, entering the wilds, a place where help may not be readily available.

When planning your hike, follow these steps:

• Print a road map showing how to reach the parking lot near the trailhead. Outline the route with a transparent yellow highlighter and write out the directions.

• Print a satellite photo of the parking area and the trailhead. Mark the trailhead on the photo.

• Print a topo map of the trail. Outline the trail with the yellow highlighter. Note interesting features you want to see along the trail and the destination.

• If carrying GPS, program this information into your device.

• Make a timeline for your trip, listing: when you will leave home; when you will arrive at the trailhead; your turn back time; when you will return for home in your vehicle; and when you will arrive at your home.

• Estimate how much water and food you will need to bring based on the amount of time you plan to spend on the trail and in your vehicle. You'll need at least two pints of water per person for every hour on the trail.

• Fill out two copies of a hiker's safety form. Leave one in your vehicle.

• Share all of this information with a responsible person remaining in civilization, leaving a hiker's safety form with them. If they do not hear from you within an hour of when you plan to leave the trail in your vehicle, they should contact authorities to report you as possibly lost.

Clothing

Footwear

If your feet hurt, the hike is over, so getting the right footwear is worth the time. Making sure the footwear fits before hitting the trail also is a good idea. With children, if you've gone a few weeks without hiking, that's plenty of time for feet to grow, and they may have just outgrown their hiking boots. Check out everyone's footwear a few days before head-ing out on the hike. If it doesn't fit, replace it.

For flat, smooth, dry trails, sneakers and cross-trainers are fine, but if you really want to head onto less traveled roads or tackle areas that aren't typically dry, you'll need hiking boots. Once you start doing any rocky or steep trails – and remember that a trail you consider moderately steep needs to be only half that angle for a child to consider it extremely steep – you'll want hiking boots, which offer rugged tread perfect for hand-ling rough trails.

Socks

Socks serve two purposes: to wick sweat away from skin and to provide cushioning. Cotton socks aren't very good for hiking, except in extremely dry environments, because they retain moisture that can lead to blisters. Wool socks or liner socks work best. You'll want to look for three-season socks, also known as trekking socks. While a little thicker than summer socks, their extra cushioning generally prevents blisters. Also, make sure kids don't put on holey socks; that's just inviting blisters.

Layering

On all but hot, dry days, when hiking you should wear multiple layers of clothing that provide various levels of protection against sweat, heat loss, wind and potentially rain. Layering works because the type of clothing you select for each stratum serves a different function, such as wicking moisture or shielding against wind. In addition, trapped air between each layer of clothing is warmed by your body heat. Layers also can be added or taken off as needed.

Generally, you need three layers. Closest to your skin is the wicking layer, which pulls perspiration away from the body and into the next layer, where it evaporates. Exertion from walking means you will sweat and generate heat, even if the weather is cold. The second layer provides insulation, which helps keep you warm. The last layer is a water-resistant shell that protects you from rain, wind, snow and sleet.

As the seasons and weather change, so does the type of clothing you select for each layer. The first layer ought to be a loose-fitting T-shirt in summer, but in winter and on other cold days you might opt for a long-sleeved moisture-wicking synthetic material, like polypropylene. During winter, the next layer probably also should cover the neck, which often is exposed to the elements. A turtleneck works fine, but preferably not one made of cotton. The third layer in winter, depending on the temperature, could be a wool sweater, a half-zippered long sleeved fleece jacket, or a fleece vest.

You might even add a fourth layer of a hooded parka with pockets, made of material that can block wind and resist water. Gloves or mittens as well as a hat also are necessary on cold days.

Headgear

Half of all body heat is lost through the head, hence the hiker's adage, "If your hands are cold, wear a hat." In cool, wet weather, wearing a hat is at least good for avoiding hypothermia, a potentially deadly condition in which heat loss occurs faster than the body can generate it. Children are more susceptible to hypothermia than adults.

Especially during summer, a hat with a wide brim is useful in keeping the sun out of eyes. It's also nice should rain start falling.

For young children, get a hat with a chin strap. They like to play with their hats, which will fly off in a wind gust if not fastened some way to the child.

Sunglasses

Sunglasses are an absolute must if walking through open areas exposed to the sun and in winter when you can suffer from snow blindness. Look for 100% UV-protective shades, which provide the best screen.

Equipment

A couple of principles should guide your purchases. First,

the longer and more complex the hike, the more equipment you'll need. Secondly, your general goal is to go light. Since you're on a day hike, the amount of gear you'll need is a fraction of what backpackers shown in magazines and catalogues usually carry. Still, the inclination of most day hikers is to not carry enough equipment. For the lightness issue, most gear today is made with titanium and siliconized nylon, ensuring it is sturdy yet fairly light. While the following list of what you need may look long, it won't weigh much.

Backpacks

Sometimes called daypacks (for day hikes or for kids), backpacks are essential to carry all of the essentials you need – snacks, first-aid kit, extra clothing.

For day hiking, you'll want to get yourself an internal frame, in which the frame giving the backpack its shape is inside the pack's fabric so it's not exposed to nature. Such frames usually are lightweight and comfortable. External frames have the frame outside the pack, so they are exposed to the elements. They are excellent for long hikes into the backcountry when you must carry heavy loads.

As kids get older, and especially after they've been hiking for a couple of years, they'll want a "real" backpack. Unfortunately, most backpacks for kids are overbuilt and too heavy. Even light ones that safely can hold up to 50 pounds are inane for most children.

When buying a daypack for your child, look for sternum straps, which help keep the strap on the shoulders. This is vital for prepubescent children, as they do not have the broad shoulders that come with adolescence, meaning packs likely will slip off and onto their arms, making them uncomfortable and difficult to carry. Don't buy a backpack that a child will "grow into." Backpacks that don't fit well simply will lead to sore shoulder and back muscles and could result in poor posture.

Also, consider purchasing a daypack with a hydration system for kids. This will help ensure they drink a lot of water. More on this later when we get to canteens.

Before hitting the trail, always check your children's backpacks to make sure that they have not overloaded them. Kids think they need more than they really do. They also tend to overestimate their own ability to carry stuff. Sibling rivalries often lead to children packing more than they should in their rucksacks, too. Don't let them overpack "to teach them a lesson," though, as it can damage bones and turn the hike into a bad experience.

A good rule of thumb is no more than 25 percent capacity. Most upper elementary school kids can carry only about 10 pounds for any short distance. Subtract the weight of the backpack, and that means only 4-5 pounds in the backpack. Overweight children will need to carry a little less than this or they'll quickly be out of breath.

Child carriers

You'll have to carry infant and toddlers. Until infants can hold their heads up, which usually doesn't happen until about four to six months of age, a front pack (like a Snugli or Baby Bjorn) is best. It keeps the infant close for warmth and balances out your backpack. At the same time, though, you must watch for baby overheating in a front pack, so you'll need to remove the infant from your body at rest stops.

Once children reach about 20 pounds, they typically can hold their heads up and sit on their own. At that point, you'll want a baby carrier (sometimes called a child carrier or baby backpack), which can transfer the infant's weight to your hips when you walk. You'll not only be comfortable, but your child will love it, too.

Look for a baby carrier that is sturdy yet lightweight. Your child is going to get heavier as time passes, so about the only way you can counteract this is to reduce the weight of the items you use to carry things. The carrier also should have adjustment points, as you don't want your child to outgrow the carrier too soon. A padded waist belt and padded shoulder straps are necessary for your comfort. The carrier should provide some kind of head and neck support if you're hauling an infant. It also should offer back support for children of all ages, and leg holes should be wide enough so there's no chafing. You want to be able to load your infant without help, so it should be stable enough to stand that way when you take it off the child can sit in it for a moment while you get turned around. Stay away from baby carriers with only shoulder straps as you need the waist belt to help shift the child's weight to your hips for more comfortable walking.

Fanny packs

Also known as a belt bag, a fanny pack is virtually a must for anyone with a baby carrier, as you can't otherwise lug a backpack. If your significant other is with you, he or she can carry the backpack, of course. Still, the fanny pack also is a good alternative to a backpack in hot weather, as it will reduce back sweat.

If you have only one or two kids on a hike, or if they also are old enough to carry daypacks, your fanny pack need not be large. A mid-size pouch can carry at least 200 cubic inches of supplies, which is more than enough to accommodate all the materials you need. A good fanny pack also has a spot for hooking canteens to.

Canteens

Canteens or plastic bottles filled with water are vital for any hike, no matter how short the trail. You'll need to have enough of them to carry about two pints of water per person for every hour of hiking.

Trekking poles

Also known as walking poles or walking sticks, trekking poles are necessary for maintaining stability on uneven or wet surfaces and to help reduce fatigue. The latter makes them useful on even surfaces. By transferring weight to the arms, a trekking pole can reduce stress on your knees and lower back, allowing you to maintain a better posture and to go farther.

If an adult with a baby or toddler on your back, you'll primarily want a trekking pole to help you maintain your balance, even if on a flat surface, and to help absorb some of the impact of your step.

Graphite tips provide the best traction. A basket just above the tip is a good idea so the stick doesn't sink into mud or sand. Angled cork handles are ergonomic and help absorb sweat from your hands so they don't blister. A strap on the handle to wrap around your hand is useful so the stick doesn't slip out. Telescopic poles are a good idea as you can adjust them as needed based on the terrain you're hiking and as kids grow to accommodate their height.

The pole also needs to be sturdy enough to handle rugged terrain, as you don't want a pole that bends when you press it to the ground. Spring-loaded shock absorbers help when heading down a steep incline but aren't necessary. Indeed, for a short walk across flat terrain, the right length stick is about all you need.

Carabiners

Carabiners are metal loops, vaguely shaped like a D, with a sprung or screwed gate. You'll find that hooking a couple of them to your backpack or fanny pack useful in many ways. For example, if you need to dig through a fanny pack, you can hook the strap of your trekking pole to it. Your hat, camera straps, first-aid kit, and a number of other objects also can connect to them. Hook carabiners to your fanny pack or backpack upon purchasing them so you don't forget them when packing. Small carabiners with sprung gates are inexpensive, but they do have a limited life span of a couple of dozen hikes.

Navigational Tools
Paper maps

Paper maps may sound passé in this age of GPS, but you'll find the variety and breadth of view they offer to be useful. During the planning process, a paper map (even if viewing it online), will be far superior to a GPS device. On the hike, you'll also want a backup to GPS. Or like many casual hikers, you may not own GPS at all, which makes paper maps indispensable.

Standard road maps (which includes printed guides and handmade trail maps) show highways and locations of cities and parks. Maps included in guidebooks, printed guides handed out at parks, and those that are hand-drawn tend to be designed like road maps, and often carry the same positives and negatives.

Topographical maps give contour lines and other important details for crossing a landscape. You'll find them invaluable on a hike into the wilds. The contour lines' shape and their spacing on a topo map show the form and steepness of a hill or bluff, unlike the standard road map and most brochures and hand-drawn trail maps. You'll also know if you're in a woods, which is marked in green, or in a clearing, which is marked in white. If you get lost, figuring out where you are and how to get to where you need to be will be much easier with such information.

Aerial photos offer a view from above that is rendered exactly as it would look from an airplane. Thanks to Google and other online services, you can get fairly detailed pictures of the landscape. Such pictures are an excellent resource when researching a hiking trail. Unfortunately, those pictures don't label what a feature is or what it's called, as would a topo map. Unless there's a stream, determining if a feature is a valley bottom or a ridgeline also can be difficult. Like topo maps, satellite and aerial photos can be out of date a few years.

GPS

By using satellites, the global positioning system can find your spot on the Earth to within 10 feet. With a GPS device, you can preprogram the trailhead location and mark key turns and landmarks as well as the hike's end point. This mobile map is a powerful technological tool that almost certainly ensures you won't get lost – so long as you've correctly programmed the information. GPS also can calculate travel time and act as a compass, a barometer and altimeter, making such devices virtually obsolete on a hike.

In remote areas, however, reception is spotty at best for GPS, rendering your mobile map worthless. A GPS device also runs on batteries, and there's always a chance they will go dead. Or you may drop your device, breaking it in the process. Their screens are small, and sometimes you need a large paper map to get a good sense of the natural landmarks around you.

Compass

Like a paper map, a compass is indispensable even if you use GPS. Should your GPS no longer function, the compass then can be used to tell you which direction you're heading. A protractor compass is best for hiking. Beneath the compass needle is a transparent base with lines to help your orient yourself. The compass often serves as a magnifying glass to help you make out map details. Most protractor compasses also come with a lanyard for easy carrying.

Food and Water

Water

As water is the heaviest item you'll probably carry, there is a temptation to not take as much as one should. Don't skimp on the amount of water you bring, though; after all, it's the one supply your body most needs. It's always better to end up having more water than needed than returning to your vehicle dehydrated.

How much water should you take? Adults need at least a quart for every two hours hiking. Children need to drink about a quart every two hours of walking and more if the weather is hot or dry. To keep kids hydrated, have them drink at every rest stop.

Don't presume there will be water on the hiking trail. Most trails outside of urban areas lack such an amenity. In addition, don't drink water from local streams, lakes, rivers or ponds. There's no way to tell if local water is safe or not. As soon as you have consumed half of your water supply, you should turn around for the vehicle.

Food

Among the many wonderful things about hiking is that

snacking between meals isn't frowned upon. Unless going on an all-day hike in which you'll picnic along the way, you want to keep everyone in your hiking party fed, especially as hunger can lead to lethargic and discontented children. It'll also keep young kids from snacking on the local flora or dirt. Before hitting the trail, you'll want to repackage as much of the food as possible as products sold at grocery stores tend to come in bulky packages that take up space and add a little weight to your backpack. Place the food in re-sealable plastic bags.

Bring a variety of small snacks for rest stops. You don't want kids filling up on snacks, but you do need them to maintain their energy levels if they're walking or to ensure they don't turn fussy if riding in a child carrier. Go for complex carbo-hy-drates and proteins for maintaining energy. Good options in-clude dried fruits, jerky, nuts, peanut butter, prepared energy bars, candy bars with a high protein content (nuts, peanut but-ter), crackers, raisins and trail mix (called "gorp"). A num-ber of trail mix recipes are available online; you and your child-ren may want to try them out at home to see which ones you col-lectively like most.

Salty treats rehydrate better than sweet treats do. Chocolate and other sweets are fine if they're not all that's served, but re-member they also tend to lead to thirst and to make sticky messes. Whichever snacks you choose, don't experiment with food on the trail. Bring what you know kids will like.

Give the first snack within a half-hour of leaving the trailhead or you risk children becoming tired and whiny from low energy levels. If kids start asking for them every few steps even after having something to eat at the last rest stop, consider timing snacks to reaching a seeable landmark, such as, "We'll get out the trail mix when we reach that bend up ahead."

Milk for infants

If you have an infant or unweaned toddler with you, milk is as necessary as water. Children who only drink breastfed milk but don't have their mother on the hike require that you have breast-pumped milk in an insulated beverage container (such as a Thermos) that can keep it cool to avoid spoiling. Know how much the child drinks and at what frequency so you can bring enough. You'll also need to carry the child's bottle and feeding nipples. Bring enough extra water in your canteen so you can wash out the bottle after each feeding. A handkerchief can be used to dry bottles between feedings.

Don't forget the baby's pacifier. Make sure it has a string and hook attached so it connects to the baby's outfit and isn't lost.

What not to bring

Avoid soda and other caffeinated beverages, alcohol, and energy pills. The caffeine will dehydrate children as well as you. Alcohol has no place on the trail; you need your full faculties when making decisions and driving home. Energy pills essentially are a stimulant and like alcohol can lead to bad calls. If you're tired, get some sleep and hit the trail another day.

First-aid Kit

After water, this is the most essential item you can carry.

A first-aid kit should include:
- Adhesive bandages of various types and sizes, especially butterfly bandages (for younger kids, make sure they're colorful kid bandages)
- Aloe vera
- Anesthetic (such as Benzocaine)
- Antacid (tablets)

- Antibacterial (aka antibiotic) ointment (such as Neosporin or Bacitracin)
- Anti-diarrheal tablets (for adults only, as giving this to a child is controversial)
- Anti-itch cream or calamine lotion
- Antiseptics (such as hydrogen peroxide, iodine or Betadine, Mercuroclear, rubbing alcohol)
- Baking soda
- Breakable (or instant) ice packs
- Cotton swabs
- Disposable syringe (w/o needle)
- Epipen (if children or adults have allergies)
- Fingernail clippers (your multi-purpose tool might have this, and if so you can dispense with it)
- Gauze bandage
- Gauze compress pads (2x2 individually wrapped pad)
- Hand sanitizer (use this in place of soap)
- Liquid antihistamine (not Benadryl tablets, however, as children should take liquid not pills; be aware that liquid antihistamines may cause drowsiness)
- Medical tape
- Moisturizer containing an anti-inflammatory
- Mole skin
- Pain reliever (aka aspirin; for children's pain relief, use liquid acetaminophen such Tylenol or liquid ibuprofen; never give aspirin to a child under 12)
- Poison ivy cream (for treatment)
- Poison ivy soap
- Powdered sports drinks mix or electrolyte additives
- Sling
- Snakebite kit
- Thermometer

- Tweezers (your multi-purpose tool may have this allowing you to dispense with it)
- Water purification tablets

If infants are with you, be sure to also carry teething ointment (such as Orajel) and diaper rash treatment.

Many of the items should be taken out of their store packaging to make placement in your fanny pack or backpack easier. In addition, small amounts of some items – such as baking soda and cotton swabs – can be placed inside re-sealable plastic bags, since you won't need the whole amount purchased.

Make sure the first-aid items are in a waterproof container. A re-sealable plastic zipper bag is perfectly fine. As northern Minnesota sports a humid climate, be sure to replace the adhesive bandages every couple of months, as they can deteriorate in the moistness. Also, check your first-aid kit every few trips and after any hike in which you've just used it, so that you can restock used components and to make sure medicines haven't expired.

If you have older elementary-age kids and teenagers who've been trained in first aid, giving them a kit to carry as well as yourself is a good idea. Should they find themselves lost or if you cannot get to them for a few moments, the kids might need to provide very basic first aid to one another.

Hiking with Children: Attitude Adjustment

To enjoy hiking with kids, you'll first have to adopt your child's perspective. Simply put, we must learn to hike on our kids' schedules – even though they may not know that's what we're doing.

Compared to adults, kids can't walk as far, they can't walk as fast, and they will grow bored more quickly. Every step we take requires three for them. In addition, early walkers, up to two years of age, prefer to wander than to "hike." Preschool kids will start to walk the trail, but at a rate of only about a mile per hour. With stops, that can turn a three-mile hike into a four-hour journey. Kids also won't be able to hike as steep of trails as you or handle as inclement of weather as you might.

This all may sound limiting, especially to long-time backpackers used to racking up miles or bagging peaks on their hikes, but it's really not. While you may have to put off some backcountry and mountain climbing trips for a while, it also opens to you a number of great short trails and nature hikes with spectacular sights that you may have otherwise skipped because they weren't challenging enough.

So sure, you'll have to make some compromises, but the payout is high. You're not personally on the hike to get a workout but to spend quality time with your children.

Family Dog

Dogs are part of the family, and if you have children, they'll want to share the hiking experience with their pets. In turn, dogs will have a blast on the trail, some larger dogs can be used as Sherpas, and others will defend against threatening animals.

But there is a downside to dogs. Many will chase animals and so run the risk of getting lost or injured. Also, a doggy bag will have to be carried for dog pooh – yeah, it's natural, but also inconsiderate to leave for other hikers to smell and for their kids to step in. In addition, most dogs almost always will lose a battle against a threatening animal, so there's a price to be paid for your safety.

Many places where you'll hike solve the dilemma for you as dogs aren't allowed on their trails. Dogs are verboten on some parks trails but usually permitted on those in national forests. Always check with the park ranger before heading to the trail.

If you can bring a dog, make sure it is well behaved and friendly to others. You don't need your dog biting another hiker while unnecessarily defending the family.

Rules of the Trail

Ah, the woods or a wide open meadow, peaceful and quiet, not a single soul around for miles. Now you and your children can do whatever you want.

Not so fast.

Act like wild animals on a hike, and you'll destroy the very aspects of the wilds that make them so attractive. You're also likely to end up back in civilization, specifically an emergency room. And there are other people around. Just as you would wish them to treat you courteously, so you and your children should do the same for them.

Let's cover how to act civilized on the trail.

Minimize damage to your surroundings

When on the trail, follow the maxim of "Leave no trace." Obviously, you shouldn't toss litter on the ground, start rockslides, or pollute water supplies. How much is damage and how much is good-natured exploring is a gray area, of course. Most serious backpackers will say you should never pick up objects, break branches, throw rocks, pick flowers, and so on – the idea is not to disturb the environment at all.

Good luck getting a four-year-old to think like that. The good news is a four-year-old won't be able to throw around many rocks or break most branches.

Still, children from their first hike into the wilderness should be taught to respect nature and to not destroy their environment. While you might overlook a preschooler hurling rocks into a puddle, they can be taught to sniff rather than pick flowers. As they grow older, you can teach them the value of leaving the rock alone. Regardless of age, don't allow children to write on boulders or carve into trees.

Many hikers split over picking berries. To strictly abide by the "minimize damage" principle, you wouldn't pick any berries at all. Kids, however, are likely to find great pleasure in eating blackberries, currants and thimbleberries as ambling down the trail. Personally, I don't see any problem enjoying a few berries if the long-term payoff is a respect and love for nature. To minimize damage, teach them to only pick berries they can reach from the trail so they don't trample plants or deplete food supplies for animals. They also should only pick what they'll eat.

Collecting is another issue. In national and most state and county parks, taking rocks, flower blossoms and even pine cones is illegal. Picking flowers moves many species, especially if they are rare and native, one step closer to extinction. Archeological ruins are extremely fragile, and even touching them can damage a site.

But on many trails, especially gem trails, collecting is part of the adventure. Use common sense – if the point of the trail is to find materials to collect, such as a gem trail, take judiciously, meaning don't overcollect. Otherwise, leave it there.

Sometimes the trail crosses private land. If so, walking around fields, not through them, always is best or you could damage a farmer's crops.

Pack out what you pack in

Set the example as a parent: Don't litter yourself; whenever stopping, pick up whatever you've dropped; and always require kids to pick up after themselves when they litter. In the spirit of "Leave no trace," try to leave the trail cleaner than you found it, so if you come across litter that's safe to pick up, do so and bring it back to a trash bin in civilization. Given this, you may want to bring a plastic bag to carry out garbage.

Picking up litter doesn't just mean gum and candy wrappers but also some organic materials that take a long time to decompose and aren't likely to be part of the natural environment you're hiking. In particular, these include peanut shells, orange peelings, and eggshells. Burying litter, by the way, isn't viable. Either animals or erosion soon will dig it up, leaving it scattered around the trail and woods.

Stay on the trail

Hiking off trail means potentially damaging fragile growth. Following this rule not only ensures you minimize damage but is also a matter of safety. Off trail is where kids most likely will encounter dangerous animals and poisonous plants. Not being able to see where they're stepping also increases the likelihood of falling and injuring themselves. Leaving the trail raises the chances of getting lost. Staying on the trail also means staying out of caves, mines or abandoned structures you may encounter. They are usually dangerous places.

Finally, never let children take a shortcut on a switchback trail. Besides putting them on steep ground upon which they could slip, their impatient act causes the switchback to erode.

Trail Dangers

On Voyageur National Park trails, three common dangers face hikers – ticks, bears and poison ivy/sumac. Fortunately, these threats are easily avoidable.

Ticks

One of the greatest dangers comes from the smallest of

creatures: ticks. Both the wood and the deer tick can infect people with Lyme disease.

Ticks usually leap onto people from the top of a grass blade as you brush against it, so walking in the middle of the trail away from high plants is a good idea. Wearing a hat, a long sleeve shirt tucked into pants, and pants tucked into shoes or socks, also will keep ticks off you, though this is not foolproof as they sometimes can hook onto clothing. A tightly woven cloth provides the best protection, however. Children can pick up a tick that has hitchhiked onto the family dog, so outfit Rover and Queenie with a tick-repelling collar.

After hiking into an area where ticks live, you'll want to examine your children's bodies (as well as your own) for them. Check warm, moist areas of the skin, such as under the arms, the groin and head hair. Wearing light-colored clothing helps make the tiny tick easier to spot.

To get rid of a tick that has bitten you or another in your hiking party, drip either disinfectant or rubbing alcohol on the bug, so it will loosen its grip. Grip the tick close to its head, slowly pulling it away from the skin. This hopefully will prevent it from releasing saliva that spreads disease. Rather than kill the tick, keep it in a plastic bag so that medical professionals can analyze it should disease symptoms appear.

Next, wash the bite area with soap and water then apply antiseptic.

In the days after leaving the woods, also check for signs of disease from ticks. Look for bulls-eye rings, a sign of a Lyme disease. Other symptoms include a large red rash, joint pain, and flu-like symptoms.

If any of these symptoms appear, seek medical attention immediately. Fortunately, antibiotics exist to cure most tick-related diseases.

Bears

Bears are a rare sight but still a potential danger at Voyageurs National Park. Avoidance always is a better solution than being forced into a situation where you have to scare off an attacking bear. You can avoid them by staying out of bear areas in spring when they're awaking from hibernation or tending cubs. Typically bears will avoid us, but a mother who thinks her cubs are threatened more than likely will chase if not attack you. If you stumble across a bear with cubs, keep your distance and move away from them. Sometimes the mother will send her cubs up a tree as she watches to see if you are a threat; don't pass between her and that tree, or she'll attack.

Also, avoid berry patches in fall. If you notice signs of bears, like paw prints, droppings, demolished berry bushes, claw marks on trees, or the smell of carrion, you shouldn't continue onward.

If you do encounter a lone bear, don't turn your back to it but gather everyone in the group together in a single cluster, make as much noise as possible, and move slowly in opposite direction. Bears usually won't attack a group of more than four people.

Should you accidentally come face to face with a bear, you can try to scare it off. Jingling bells work well. You also can throw rocks at ground in front of the bear if it approaches, but this probably necessitates that you bend down, making you an easier target for a fast-moving animal. Pepper spray also will ward off a bear and can be conveniently holstered so it's easy to reach and use.

If attacked, don't run but play dead by lying on the ground, bringing your legs to your chest, tucking in your head, and covering the back of your neck with your hands. The bear might swat and sniff at you, but when it sees you're playing dead, it won't consider you a threat.

Poison ivy/sumac

Often the greatest danger in the wilds isn't our own clumsiness or foolhardiness but various plants we encounter. The good news is that we mostly have to force the encounter with flora.

Touching the leaves of either poison ivy or poison sumac in particular results in an itchy, painful rash. Each plant's sticky resin, which causes the reaction, clings to clothing and hair, so you may not have "touched" a leaf, but once your hand runs against the resin on shirt or jeans, you'll probably get the rash.

To avoid touching these plants, you'll need to be able to identify each one. Remember the "Leaves of three, let it be" rule for poison ivy. Besides groups of three leaflets, poison ivy has shiny green leaves that are red in spring and fall. Poison sumac's leaves are not toothed as are non-poisonous sumac, and in autumn their leaves turn scarlet. Be forewarned that even after leaves fall off, poison oak's stems can carry some of the itchy resin.

By staying on the trail and walking down its middle rather than the edges, you are unlikely to come into contact with this pair of irritating plants. That probably is the best preventative. Poison ivy barrier creams also can be helpful, but they only temporarily block the resin. This lulls you into a false sense of safety, and so you may not bother to watch for poison ivy.

To treat poison ivy/sumac, wash the part of the body that has touched the plant with poison ivy soap and cold water. This will erode the oily resin, so it'll be easier to rinse off. If you don't have any of this special soap, plain soap sometimes will work if used within a half-hour of touching the plant. Apply a poison ivy cream and get medical attention immediately. Wearing gloves, remove any clothing (including shoes) that has touched the plants, washing them and the worn gloves right away.

For more about these topics and many others, pick up this author's "Hikes with Tykes: A Practical Guide to Day Hiking with Kids." You also can find tips online at the author's "Day Hiking Trails" blog at *hikeswithtykes.blogspot.com*. Have fun on the trail!

Bonus Section II: National Parks Primer

The breadth of wonders at America's national parks astounds the mind. You can stand at the nation's rooftop with 60 peaks taller than 12,000 feet at Rocky Mountain National Park or in a gash more than a mile deep in the earth at Grand Canyon. You can visit among the driest places in the world where little more than an inch of rain falls per year upon the beige sands of Death Valley or step into the ocean itself, such as Biscayne National Park where the bulk of the wilderness is the Atlantic and its vibrantly colored coral reefs. You can see some of the oldest rock on Earth, like the 1.2 billion year-old granite at Shenandoah National Park, to some of the newest land on the planet, as at Hawai'i Volcanoes National Park where you can watch lava flows create new ground inch by inch before you. You can enjoy parks that are primarily historical and even urban in nature, such as Cuyahoga Valley National Park, which features pioneer farms and bicycle paths, while others preserve breathless, awe-inspiring tracts of wilderness and stone, such as Yosemite's El Capitan and Half Dome. You can trek through caves with rooms larger than a foot-ball field situated hundreds of feet below the ground, such as at Carlsbad Caverns, or beneath trees soaring 15 stories over your head at Redwood National Park.

Given these grand wonders, not surprisingly national parks are a major travel destination. Indeed, many parks report record attendance during past few years. In 2017, annual attendance at parks operated by the National Parks Service hit 331 million visits – falling just short of its record number of visits set the previous year.

But with so many sights and given most national parks' distance from major population centers, how can visitors be sure they'll make the best use of their time and see all of the highlights?

Unfortunately, many park visitors treat a national park like a drive-in theater. Fully experiencing any nat-ional park requires that you "get out of the car," though. As W.H. Davies once wrote, "Now shall I walk/Or shall I ride?/'Ride,' Pleasure said; 'Walk,' Joy replied." A day hike can deliver the joy that each park offers.

What is (and isn't) a national park

Often local tourism agencies and business groups will refer to the "national park" near their community. If you've done any amount of traveling, such statements on websites and brochures would lead you to believe that there are hundreds of national parks!

The truth of that matter is that many of those agen-cies and hometown boosters actually are referring to units admin-istered by the National Park Service. The park service oversees more than 400 units, of which only 59 are actual national parks.

The types of units the park service manages are broken into more than 20 categories. Among the more common ones are national historical parks, national historic sites, national mon-uments, national memorials, national military parks, national battlefield parks, national battlefield sites, national battlefields, national preserves, and national reserves.

Other agencies also run parklands set aside for public use. The U.S. Forest Service overseas national forests. States and counties typically manage what are smaller versions of nat-ional parks and national forests. The U.S. Fish and Wildlife Ser-vice handles wildlife refuges while the Bureau of Land Manage-ment is in charge of wilderness areas.

As national forests and state parks adjoin national parks, travelers may not know when they've entered one unit or left another. Sometimes these different units even are operated as a single park, as is the case with the array of public lands pro-tecting redwoods in north-western California, to save costs.

National parks generally are considered the crown jewels of the park service's outdoor experiences. When visiting a nat-ional park, though, don't discount the surrounding state parks, national forests, and other recreational areas, as they also offer excellent sights to see. They're also often less crowded than a national park.

Choosing a park to visit

Planning a trip to a national park isn't like going to the mall. Unless you're lucky enough to live near a nat-ional park, any trip to one will be part of a vacation for you and your family. So you'll need to choose which park you want to visit.

Your interests

Begin by asking what you'd most like to see. Do you want to watch wildlife? Experience great geological fea-tures like can-yons and exotic rock formations? Of des-erts, volcanoes, aut-umn leaves, or tropical rain forests, which appeals to you? Are you interested in history? Was there a park you've always wanted to visit since childhood?

The quandary you'll face is that you'll want to see more than you probably have vacation time for!

Getting there

Next, decide how you'll reach the park. Many parks are re-mote and require driving, at least from a nearby airport. How much time you have to travel and how much money you're able to spend on transportation can help you narrow your list of potential parks to visit during a vacation.

Costs

After that, determine how much money is in your budget. The good news is that the park itself is fairly in-expensive to visit. As of press time, Congaree National Park in South Car-olina and Cuyahoga Valley National Park in Ohio are absolutely free to enter while at the upper end Grand Canyon National Park charges $30 a vehicle for a week-long stay.

Sometimes fees are reduced (and even waived) for students and military personnel. Generally, the pass you purchase is good for a few days.

Many times a year, the park service offers "free entrance days." Expect the park to be crowded on those days, however, as they often coincide with holidays.

If you plan to hike national parks regularly, you should con-sider purchasing a National Parks and Federal Recreational Lands Pass, which will get a noncommercial vehicle plus pass-holder and three passengers into any national park for less than $100 a year.

Even less expensive versions of the pass are available for senior citizens, the disabled and National Park volunteers. If you visit a number of parks over several weeks, you'll definite-ly save on admission costs going this route.

Be forewarned that there may be additional fees if planning

to camp or to park an RV. Almost any hike that involves being part of a tour group at a major destination within a park carries a cost beyond the entry fee.

The real cost will come in lodging and food. Hotels within national parks generally are pricey while those near the park entrances only slight less so. Camping in the park or a neighboring national forest can be a good, inexpensive option. Food also can cost a small fortune within a park, but usually there are plenty of good, less expensive alternatives in nearby communities.

When to visit

Another consideration is when you will travel. Parts of some parks, such as Rocky Mountain, Crater Lake and Yosemite, actually cannot be reached during winter as heavy snowfall closes high mountain roads. Others, such as Death Valley, are simply too dangerous to hike in the summer heat. Most parks also have a peak season in which roads, campgrounds, sites and trails will be crowded; visiting a park when attendance is low, but the weather is ideal.

The high season typically is summer, running from Memorial Day through Labor Day weekends; those three-day weekends as well as when the Fourth of July falls on a Friday or Monday, usually draw the largest crowds in a year. In hot desert areas, the high season shifts slightly, as Death Valley and Arches national parks pull more people in late spring and early autumn when temperatures are pleasant.

The ideal time to visit is the off-season just before or just after high season. This can be difficult as usually high season coincides with when children are on school vacation.

Also think about the day of the week you will visit. You usually can avoid crowds by visiting weekdays, especially Monday through Thursday, when attendance dips. On three-day holiday weekends, sometimes the adjoining Thursday or Tuesday can see an uptick as well.

The time of day also plays a role. The earlier in the morning you can get to a national park, the less congested it will be on roadways and at popular sites. Usually, park visitors make their way from the nearest hotels mid-morning to the front gates and then set off again before sunset to their lodging. In addition, visitor centers at some parks will close for holidays, usually Christmas.

Of course, visiting during the off-season and on week-days comes with trade-offs. The weather may be cold or extremely hot; sometimes ranger-led park programs are nil on weekdays, especially in the off-season. In addition, access to some parks can be limited depending on the season. Yellowstone, for example, closes some of its entrances during winter as snowfall at the high elevations makes roads impassable. Other parks, such as Crater Lake, can't be reached at all during the off-season because of heavy snow.

Another possibility for avoiding crowds is to visit national parks that see low attendance overall. Yosemite, Yellowstone, the Grand Canyon and Cuyahoga national parks typically boast the highest attendance so definitely will be crowded during the high seasons. Great Basin (in Nevada) and Theodore Roosevelt (in North Dakota) national parks, however, are easy to reach but see few visitors compared to those in California, Arizona and Utah.

Pets

Pets are an important member of many families, and a vacation with them at a national park is possible, albeit with limitations.

Dogs and cats typically are only allowed in the park's developed areas, such as drive-in campgrounds and pic-nic areas, but rarely on trails. They also must be on a leash as well.

So if heading on a day hike, what to do with Rover or Queenie? Some parks offer kennels; short of that, one of your party will have to stay behind with the pet.

National forests surrounding the national park usu-ally have more lenient rules regarding pets, so if camp-ing you may want to consider pitching a tent there in-stead, though an adult member of the party still will have to stay with the dogs while everyone else hikes the national park.

Getting kids involved

Children obviously can benefit from visiting these great outdoors treasures. A trip to a national park will give any child fond memories that will literally last a lifetime. During their visit, they will experience their natural joy of discovery, certainly by seeing and exploring the sights themselves or perhaps through a touch table in which they get to feel fossils or a rabbit pelt at a visitor center. The visit alone will encourage their appreciation for nature. Take them on a hike through these wild areas, and they get the bonus of exercise in the fresh air.

The National Park Service offers a variety of great, interactive programs aimed at teaching kids about nature through fun and adventure. They often become the more memorable moments of a park visit for children, and a few even offer cool souvenirs at the end.

Among the programs:

• **Junior Ranger –** Most parks now offer some version of this program, in which kids by filling out a self-guided booklet and sometimes performing volunteer work can earn a Junior

Ranger patch or pin among other goodies.

• **Ranger-led activities** – Park rangers often host family-friendly activities on the park's geology, wildlife, ecology, history and other topics. Some parks during the evening offer programs in which kids can sit about a campfire and learn about nature.

• **Star parties** – Several national parks, especially those that are remote, offer nighttime viewings of the sky with telescopes. Your kids never will see a sky so brilliantly lit with stars.

• **Touch programs** – Some parks offer kids the opportunity to meet live animals or to touch cool found objects, such as turtle shells, feathers and rocks. They usually are held at the park's nature or visitor center.

Kids' activities aren't limited to just inside the park, however. Before even leaving on your trip, have your children:

• **Check out the park's website** – Many of the websites list activities specific to their park that later can be played on the drive to the park or during hikes.

• **Meet Smokey Bear virtually** – Younger kids can learn about forest fires and nature at Smokey Bear's official website: *www.smokeybear.com/kids*

• **Visit Webrangers** – Get kids excited about your trip with a stop at the Webrangers website (*www.nps.gov/webrangers*). Kids can play more than 50 online games that allow them to explore various national parks.

Hiking national parks tips

Day hiking usually isn't as simple as throwing on one's tennis shoes and hitting the trail. While that may be fine at a small city park, doing so in a national park can invite disaster. Though day hiking hardly requires as much gear or planning as a backpacking, you still need to bring some equipment and to think ahead.

Following these 10 simple guidelines should ensure your day hike is problem-free:

- **Know where you're going** – Look at a map of the trail before going out on it. Bring a paper map and com-pass with you on the trail and check both frequently as you walk.
- **Get the right footwear** – If your feet hurt, the hike is over. Good-fitting hiking boots almost always are a must on wilderness trails while cross-trainers probably are fine for paved surfaces; sandals almost always are a no-no.
- **Bring water** – You'll need about two pints of water per person for every hour of hiking and even more if in hot or dry climates. Leave soda and sugary fruit drinks at home; they are no replacement for water.
- **Layer your clothing** – Doing so allows you to remove and put back on clothing as needed to suit the weather. Make sure the layer next to the body wicks moisture away from the skin while the outer layer protects against wind and rain.
- **Carry a first-aid kit** – A small kit that allows you to bandage cuts and that contains some emergency equipment such as matches and a whistle will suffice for short hikes.
- **Don't overpack** – A lighter backpack always is better than one full of stuff you don't need. At the same time, don't skimp on the essentials so that you can safely complete the hike.
- **Use a trekking pole** – Unless the surface you're on is absolutely level, you'll find a walking stick helps reduce fatigue. This is especially true if you're carrying a backpack.
- **Follow the rules of the trail** – Leave no trace by not littering ("Pack out what you pack in.") and by staying on the trail. Don't deface rocks or destroy signage.
- **Don't forget a snack** – Trail mix as well as jerky can help you maintain energy on the trail. It's also a good motivator for

any children with you.

   • **Enjoy the journey** – Reaching the destination is never as important as having a good time on the way there. If with children, play games, pause when something grabs their attention, and never turn the hike into a death march.

Services and amenities

Services and amenities at national parks can vary greatly depending on the number of visitors and the part of the park you're in. You almost always can expect to find a visitor center and campgrounds with bathrooms; that doesn't mean there will be a restaurant or a vending machine with snacks and water on site, however.

If hoping to stay in a park lodge or at a campground, quickly make reservations; the same goes for hotels, motels and campgrounds near the park. A safe bet to ensure that a reservation can be made is make them at least six months ahead and up to a year in advance at the most popular parks.

Most parks have at least some trails available for those with disabilities to traverse. Be aware, however, that these trails may not head to a park's top sights.

Best sights to see

Which national park trails offer the best vistas? Lead to awesome waterfalls? Let you see wildlife? To enjoy fall colors? Here are some lists of the best national park trails for those and many other specific interests.

Beaches

Come summertime, there's almost no better place to be than the beach. The warmth of the sun upon your face, the sound of waves splashing against the shore, the blue water stretching into the horizon...Let's go!

Among the most beautiful beaches you can visit are those in national parks. Thousands of miles of shoreline around lakes and along oceans are protected in our parks, and just like the wildlife and rock formations you're apt to find in most of them the beaches won't disappoint either.

Here are six must-see beaches at our national parks.

Ocean Path Trail, Acadia National Park: Cobble beaches and hard bedrock make up most of the shoreline for the Atlantic Ocean that surrounds the Maine park's many islands. A rare exception is the 4.4-miles round trip Ocean Path Trail that heads from a sand beach to sea cliffs.

Convoy Point, Biscayne National Park: This boardwalk trail is flat and easy, running along the Florida mangrove shore known as Convoy Point. You'll follow the blue-green waters of Biscayne Bay and be able to spot some small, mangrove-covered islands. Bring a lunch; there's a picnic area below palms overlooking the bay. Part of the boardwalk also takes you out over the water. As the bay is shallow and quite clear, you'll have no trouble spotting the bottom.

Swiftcurrent Lake, Glacier National Park: The first 0.6 miles of the trail at this Montana park heads through an evergreen forest with several short spur trails leading to beaches along Swiftcurrent Lake. Meltwater from Grinnell Glacier feeds lake, making for an crystal clear albeit cold water.

Leigh Lake, Grand Teton National Park: Several alpine lakes perfect for a family outing sit at the Wyoming park's central String Lake Area. The 1.8-mile round trip trail heads around a shimmering blue lake through green pines with gray Mount Moran soaring in the background. During summer, enjoy a picnic on the beach and then a swim in the cool waters.

Ruby Beach Trail, Olympic National Park: The Washington park's Pacific Ocean shoreline features gushing sea stacks, piles of driftwood logs, and colorful, wave-polished stones. To enjoy all three, take the 1.4-mile Ruby Beach Trail. Some of the driftwood here has floated in from the distant Columbia River.

Coastal Trail, Redwood National Park: With more than 40 miles of pristine Pacific Ocean coastline, the northern California park is the perfect place to see tide pools and sea stacks. The latter are visible from many highway vistas but to get close up to a tide pool – a small body of saltwater that sustains many colorful sea creatures on the beach at low tide – explore the 1-mile segment (2-miles round trip) of the Coastal Trail at Enderts Beach south of Crescent City.

Fall colors

Ah, autumn – the world appears to have been repainted, as red, gold and sienna orange leaves contrast with the blue sky. For many travelers, fall is their favorite time to hit the road.

But there's more to see than the leaves. As those they fall to the ground, the landscape opens up, allowing you to spot interesting geological features or terrain that summer's green foliage keeps hidden. More animal sightings also are possible as birds migrate while mammals gorge in preparation for winter's cold. As the foliage no longer is as thick, seeing them is easier.

America's national parks offer a number of great places to experience autumn's beauty. And with summer vacation over, many of the parks will be less crowded.

Six national parks particularly deliver great autumn experiences for travelers.

Cuyahoga Falls National Park: Brandywine Falls ranks among the most popular of the Ohio park's several waterfalls. The area surrounding the falls is gorgeous in October beneath autumn leaves, and the Brandywine Gorge Trail to it is shaded

Cedar Creek and Abbey Island at Ruby Beach, Olympic National Park

almost the entire way by red maples and eastern hemlocks. With a combination of segments from the Stanford Road Metro Parks Bike and Hike Trail, the gorge trail loops 1.5 miles to the falls then back to the trailhead with several crossings of Brandywine Creek.

Great Sand Dunes National Park: Most people visit this Colorado park for the sand dunes soaring 60-plus stories in the sky. There's more to the park than dunes, though. The Montville Trail provides an excellent sample of that as it heads into the surrounding mountains. The 0.5-mile loop partially runs alongside a creek, where the golden canopy of cottonwood and aspen trees sends you to an autumn wonderland.

Great Smoky Mountains National Park: The 1-mile round trip Clingmans Dome Trail heads to the highest spot in the national park and Tennessee. Autumn leaves on the road to Clingmans Dome usually change about mid-October, offering a spectacular red, orange and yellow display. At the dome's top, views of those swaths of harvest colors can stretch for up to a hundred miles in all directions.

Hot Springs National Park: Though hardly thought of as a backcountry wilderness experience, the Arkansas park does offer a number of forested trails to enjoy. The best in autumn is the Hot Springs Mountain Trail. Heading through a beautiful mixed hardwood and pine forest, the route offers a gorgeous fall leaf display – and cooler temperatures than during muggy summer.

Shenandoah National Park: Spectacular autumn views await day hikers on the Stony Man Trail, a segment of the Appalachian National Scenic Trail. At the trail's top, you'll be rewarded with an expansive view of the Shenandoah Valley and the Massanutten and Allegheny Mountains beyond, their trees alit in harvest colors, as you breathe in clean, crisp air.

Death Valley National Park – OK, there are no autumn leaves here at all – but September's cooler temperatures ensure you actually can stand leave an air conditioned vehicle for a lot longer than a minute to experience the forbidding desert landscape. Among the best places in the California park to visit is the Golden Canyon Interpretive Trail, where you can learn to read rocks that tell the tale of how a lake once here vanished.

Romance

What are the most romantic places in the world? Paris? Hawaii? Italy?

Try a national park.

Though national parks often are thought of as places to get back to nature, they're also great spots to get a little closer to your sweetie. Among the romantic possibilities are moonbows, romantic vistas, desert oasis and incredible sunrises.

49 Palms Oasis, Joshua Tree National Park

Moonbow over waterfalls: At night during a full moon, moonbows often can be seen over waterfalls as the silvery light from the nearest heavenly body refracts off the mist. Plan a spring or early summer visit to Yosemite National Park when the moon is full. On a clear night, moonlit rainbows – called moonbows – span 2425-foot high Yosemite Fall with a trail leading right to its base.

Desert oasis: What is more romantic than midnight at the oasis? Joshua Tree National Park has a few, with the 49 Palms Oasis among the easiest to reach. The 49 Palms Oasis Trail heads 1.5-miles to stands of fan palms and water pools. Bring a blanket to lay out on the sand and a picnic basket for an evening snack under the stars.

Breathtaking vistas: For many, vistas of the Blue Ridge Mountains rank among the nation's most beautiful natural

Sunrise at Pu'u'ula'ula Summit, Haleakalā National Park

scenery. The 4-mile hike up to the summit of Old Rag Mountain via the Ridge Trail at Shenandoah National Park iṣ challenging, but the 360 degree view from the top is unparalleled, as nearly 200,000 acres of wilderness stretch below you. Twirl your beloved around in a dance so that the entire scene spins before her eyes.

Stargazing: Boasting among the darkest skies in continental America, you can see up to 7,500 stars with the naked eye – nearly four times more than is typical in a rural area – at Bryce Canyon National Park. The Piracy Point Trail, a half-mile round trip from Far View Point, leads to a picnic area overlooking a cliff perfect for stargazing. Study up on the names of a few stars in the night sky and point them out to your sweetheart.

Fruitpicking: The Park Service at Capitol Reef National Park maintains more than 3,100 trees – including cherry, apricot, peach, pear and apple – in orchards planted decades ago by Mormon pioneers. For a small fee, park visitors can pick the fruit when in season. While there's no designated trail, the Historic Fruita Orchards Walk takes you through the fruit trees near Utah Hwy. 24. Share with your beloved what you've picked at your next rest stop.

Sunrise to propose by: At 10,023 feet, Pu'u'ula'ula Summit at Haleakalā National Park offers what many consider the world's most romantic sunrise. As the sun ascends over a blanket of clouds below the summit, it colors the crater from the inside out in an incredible light show. Bring a breakfast picnic and as the new day begins, propose marriage, for the sunrise symbolizes the dawning of your life together. Since you can drive to the summit, after she says "Yes," together hike one of the trails into the crater (either the Keonehe'ehe'e Trail or the Halemau'u Trail).

Sunrises and sunsets

Nothing quite so effectively displays Mother Nature's beauty than a sunrise or sunset, those few moments each day when the world shines golden and with incredible serenity.

Some of America's best sunrises and sunsets can be seen in her national parks. They range from the where the morning light first touches America each day to romantic sunsets over tropical waters, from the subtle signal for a million bats to begin their day to incredible sunrises over the continent's deepest chasm.

Here are seven must-see sunrises and sunsets at our national parks.

First sunrise at Acadia National Park: Day hikers can walk to one of the first spots where the sun touches America each morning via the South Ridge Trail in Maine's Acadia National

Park. The trail is a 7.2-miles round trip to the top of Cadillac Mountain, which is the highest summit on the Eastern seaboard. Though the hike would be done in the dark, with moonglow and flashlights, the trail is traversable. Acadia's ancient granite peaks are among the first places in the United States where the sunrise can be seen. Be sure to bring a blanket to lay out on the cold rock and take a seat looking southeast.

Gold-lined paths at Bryce Canyon: Fairyland really does exist – it's smack dab in southcentral in Utah, where a maze of totem pole-like rock formations called hoodoos grace Bryce Canyon National Park. Hoodoos are unusual landforms in which a hard caprock slows the erosion of the softer mineral beneath it. The result is a variety of fantastical shapes. Take the Queens Garden Trail, which descends into the fantasyland of hoodoos. When hiking during the early morning, sunrise's orange glow magically lights the trail's contours.

Bat show at Carlsbad Caverns: About 1 million Mexican Freetail bats live in Carlsbad Caverns. During the day, they rest on the ceiling of Bat Cave, a passageway closed to the public. At sunset, to feed for the evening, the bats dramatically swarm out of the cave in a tornadic-like spiral, their silhouettes stretching into the distant horizon. An open-air amphitheater allows visitors to safely watch the bats' departure in an event called The Night Flight. The Chihuahuan Desert Nature Trail, a half-mile loop, also allows you to watch the bats disperse across the New Mexican desert.

Breathtaking light show at Grand Canyon: Among the Grand Canyon National Park's most spectacular sights – sunrise and sunset – can be seen within walking distance of Grand Canyon Village in Arizona. While the South Rim Trail extends several miles along the canyon edge, you only have to walk to Mather Point, where views of the canyon shift like pictures in a

Hoodoo rock formations at Bryce Canyon ampitheater

marquee at both sunrise and sunset. Another great spot that's a little less crowded is Ooh Ahh Point on the South Kaibab Trail, which is east of the village and south of Yaki Point. The aptly named Ooh Ahh Point is less than 200 feet below the rim.

100-mile views at Great Smoky Mountains: You can enjoy views of sunrises and sunsets covering up to a hundred miles on the Clingmans Dome Trail in Great Smoky Mountains National Park. How incredible are the sunsets? They can be crowded, as those hoping to photograph the stunning scenery line up 45 minutes before the sun descends.

Romantic sunsets at Biscayne National Park: A full 95 percent of Florida's Biscayne National Park sits underwater, a turquoise blue paradise laced with vividly colored coral reefs – and nothing quite says romance like a sunset over this tropical ocean. Adams Key offers a quarter-mile trail from the dock through the hardwood hammock on the island's west side; most of the route skirts the beach, where the sunset can be enjoyed.

Needles aglow at Canyonlands National Park: Clambering over boulders and ambling across strangely angled slickrock – and watching needles aglow at sunset – await on Canyonlands National Park's Slickrock Trail in southeastern Utah. The 2.9-mile loop trail generally follows a mesa rim. Plan to walk the trail about an hour or so before sunset; on the final mile, tall thin rock formations called needles fill the horizon, glowing crimson as the sun sets.

Vistas

Certainly the best memories of any trip are the great vistas enjoyed along the way. For some, the beauty of the natural scene before them ranks far above any man-made art. For others, the diminutiveness experienced upon seeing an incredible panorama is a spiritual moment.

America's national parks fortunately preserve the most impressive of these vistas. But other than a sign right at the entry road, how does one know where they are? No worries – we've compiled a list of the six best vistas at our national parks, all of which are easy to reach with short hikes.

Great Smoky Mountains National Park, Clingmans Dome: You can enjoy views of up to a hundred miles atop one of the highest points east of the Mississippi River. The 1-mile round trip Clingmans Dome Trail heads to the highest spot in Great Smoky Mountains National Park and Tennessee and the third tallest east of the Mississippi. The top rewards with an incredible 360 degree panorama. A verdant spruce-fir forest sits at the ridge tops while in autumn the leaves of hardwoods below adds swaths of harvest colors. On clear days, 100-mile views are possible.

Grand Canyon National Park, South Rim: Perhaps the

South Rim, Grand Canyon National Park

most fantastic vista in all of North America is the Grand Canyon's South Rim. Indeed, the Grand Canyon rightly defies description. Most who see it for the first time say it reminds them of a majestic painting, appropriately suggesting it's a place that only can be visualized by actually gazing at it. While the South Rim Trail extends several miles along the canyon edge, a short section east of the El Tovar Hotel offers the best views. You'll be able to see the Colorado River a mile below and an array of incredible buttes, towers and ridges and that stretch up to 10 miles away on the canyon's other side.

Yosemite National Park, Yosemite Valley: Two sweeping views of Yosemite Valley await on the Sentinel Dome and Taft Point Loop. Located south of the valley along Glacier Point Road, the trail runs 4.9-miles. Taft Point allows you to get right up to the edge of the valley rim, offering magnificent views of

Yosemite Valley below and Yosemite Fall (the tallest in North America) and El Capitan across the way. The 360 degree views from the top of Sentinel Dome – which peaks at 8127 feet – are the hike's highlight. Among the visible sights are Yosemite Valley, Half Dome, El Capitan, Yosemite Falls, North Dome, and Basket Dome.

Yellowstone National Park, Fairy Falls Trail: The multi-col-ored Grand Prismatic Spring and an array of geysers can be seen on the first 0.6 miles of Yellowstone's Fairy Falls Trail. A 400-foot stretch of the trail appropriately known as Picture Hill provides a grand vista of the spring. About 370 feet in diameter, Grand Prismatic is the largest hot spring in the United States and the third largest in the world. It reaches a depth of 121 feet. Be sure to bring polarized sunglasses. By wearing them, you can see the spring's rainbow colors reflected in the steam rising off the water. The smaller Excelsior Geyser Crater sits beyond the geological wonder.

Zion National Park, Canyon Overlook Trail: You can hike past hoodoos to a vista that affords a fantastic view of Zion National Park's famous Beehives, East Temple, the Streaked Wall, and the Towers of the Virgin, on the Canyon Overlook Trail. The 1-mile round trip of pinnacles, arches and domes feels like a walk on an alien world straight out of a science fiction film. Summer temps are cooler in the morning and late evening.

Mesa Verde National Park, Park Point: Park Point, Mesa Verde's highest spot at 8572 feet above sea level with 360 degree views, is often touted as the most impressive vista in the United States. The 0.5-mile round trip Park Point Overlook Trail takes you to the view of Montezuma and Mancos valleys, and on a clear day, you can see four states – Colorado, Utah, Arizona and New Mexico. Add 0.5-miles round trip to the fire lookout tower for additional great views.

Yosemite Falls, Yosemite National Park

Waterfalls

Nothing quite demonstrates the awesome power and beauty of Mother Nature like a waterfall – hundreds of gallons of water rushing several stories over a cliffside, the vertical stream nestled in lush greenery, the mist and droplets that splash on you at the fall's base.

Fortunately, several of our national parks preserve many of the country's most fantastic falls. Many of them are quire easy to reach via short hikes.

Yosemite Falls: If there is one waterfall that everyone absolutely must see, it's this one in California's Yosemite National Park. Actually consisting of seven waterfalls, Yosemite Falls sends water rushing 2,425 feet downward into the valley. Depending on snow melt, the falls' peak flow typically occurs in May when up to 2,400 gallons of water flow down Yosemite Falls every second.

You can hike 1.2-miles round trip to the base of North America's tallest waterfall. During spring, you may want to take the trail on a clear night when the moon is full, especially if on a romantic trip. Moonlit rainbows – called moonbows – span the waterfalls.

Queenie and Fido also can enjoy the waterfalls, as leashed dogs are allowed on the trail. Be sure that your dog is comfortable with crowds and other people, however.

Tokopah Falls: Not many travelers have heard of Tokopah Falls, but it's an incredible site. A series of cascades, it drops 1200 feet – almost the height of the Empire State Building – at California's Sequoia National Park. It's a park of tall trees and tall waterfalls. A glacier carved Tokopah Valley, leaving high gray cliff walls that cradle a meadow, creeks, and a pine and fir forest. The 3.8-mile (600 foot elevation gain) Tokopah Falls Trail leads to its namesake, which is the park's highest waterfall.

Avalanche Lake waterfalls: With melting glaciers and high mountains, waterfalls can be found aplenty in Montana's Glacier National Park. Melting glaciers feed several lakes across the park, including Avalanche Lake. Start on the Trail of the Cedars then turn off onto the Avalanche Lake Trail. The 4.7-miles round trip (505-foot gain) trail heads to Avalanche Lake, where several waterfalls from Sperry Glacier drop several hundred feet to fill the valley with its turquoise waters.

Hidden Falls: You can enjoy this waterfall and then a vista at 7200 feet elevation on Grand Teton National Parks' Hidden Falls-Inspiration Point Trail. The trail runs 3.8-miles round trip into Cascade Canyon. Though technically not a waterfall but a series of cascades running 200 feet over several multiple steps, Wyoming's Hidden Falls still impresses. Because only part of the cascades are steep, there's a lot of confusion among various sources about exactly how high the drop that looks most like

Hidden Falls, Grand Teton National Park

a waterfall actually is – some say 80 feet and others say 100. Afterward, visit Inspiration Point, a short walk from the falls.

Fairy Falls: The trail to Fairy Falls at Yellowstone National Park offers a three-for-one deal: the multi-colored Grand Prismatic Spring, an array of geysers, and the 197-foot waterfall. If going to see Old Faithful, this is a perfect nearby trail to hike the same day. The 5.6-mile hike begins with geysers then arrives Grand Prismatic Spring, a wonder that boasts multicolored rings of algae. Fairy Falls comes next. The waterfalls' base supports a variety of vegetation. If looking for a place to picnic, the rocks downstream from the falls where raspberry bushes grow make a perfect spot.

Marymere Falls: A trail through a lush, old growth forest that ends at this waterfall will delight anyone hiking the Marymere Falls Trail at Olympic National Park in Washington. The 1.6-mile round trip trail really is like taking two entirely different hikes in one. Most of the trail heads through a intensely green Pacific Northwest rain forest while the last portion at the destination is purely about the waterfalls. Marymere Falls is about 90 feet high, and you'll get really close to it as the trail passes the small plunge pool. Hikers also can take a stairs to see the falls' upper segment. A few landings on the stairs offers fantastic views of the falls from different angles.

Laurel Falls: Though Rainbow Falls is the tallest at Great Smoky Mountains National Park, many visitors eschew it because of the strenuous hike. One that's much easier to reach and still spectacular in its own right is Tennessee's 80-foot Laurel Falls. The Laurel Falls Trail runs 2.6-miles round trip through a pine-oak woods with hemlock and beech along the stream, making for a colorful walk in autumn. May also is impressive, as mountain laurel blooms along the trail and near the falls, which runs its highest that month. Deer, often with fawns, wood squirrels, and songbirds are common on the trail. The waterfall on Laurel Branch consists of an upper and a lower section. A wide walkway crosses the stream where the mist from the falls roils over her head.

Brandywine Falls: This 65-foot waterfalls awaits visitors on the Brandywine Gorge Trail at Ohio's Cuyahoga Valley National Park. The Brandywine Gorge Trail loops 1.5 miles to the falls then back to the trailhead with several crossings of Brandywine Creek. The area surrounding the falls is gorgeous in October beneath autumn leaves, but the trail can be hiked any season. It's shaded almost the entire way by red maples with eastern hemlocks and green moss upon the ground once closer to the falls.

Wildflowers
From rare California poppies to sweet-scented phlox, wild-

Catawba rhododendron blooms, Great Smoky Mountains National Park

flowers begin to bloom this month across much of the country. Filling green meadows, desert basins, and forest floors, wildflowers bring a special beauty that usually can only be seen for a few weeks.

Our national parks rank among the best places to enjoy wildflowers. As those parks cover wide swaths of protected land, they offer ample area for massive blooms, enhancing the already beautiful scenery.

Here are six not-to-miss spots at our national parks for spotting wildflowers from now through summer.

Pinnacles National Park: Each spring, brilliant orange California poppies, lavender-colored bush lupine, and white mariposa lilies blossom across the nation's newest national park. To see a variety of them at different elevations and from a number of vistas, take the High Peaks and Bear Gulch trails.

Great Smoky Mountains National Park: About the same time on the other side of the continent, the forest floor on the Mingus Creek Trail turns fragrant with the pleasant sent of blue phlox. Several other shade-loving flowers also can be found along the creek, including violets, Virginia bluebells and white trillium. During late April, expect to see flame azalea in bloom on the Deep Creek/Indian Falls trails. In May, look for mountain laurel, and in June for rhododendron.

Glacier National Park: From late June through early August, summer wildflower blooms are at their peak. Check out the Swiftcurrent Lake Loop Trail for meadows strewn with purple asters, white torch-shaped clusters of beargrass, and sun yellow glacier lilies, all with majestic mountains as a backdrop.

Sequoia National Park: Next to the world's largest trees are blossoms that somehow manage to stand out despite their size. On the Crescent Meadow Trail in early July, lavender Mustang clover with yellow centers look like little pins of brilliant light against the immense pine cones that have fallen into the grass.

Crater Lake National Park: Wildflowers usually bloom along the stream next to the Annie Creek Trail and across the meadows from mid-July through August. Among those that might be spotted are Macloskey's violet, big huckleberry, sulphur flower, Crater Lake currant, western mountain ash, and wax currant.

Great Basin National Park: Amid the high desert is an oasis of summer wildflowers on the Alpine Lakes Trail. Spring-fed Lehman Creek flows into a lake and supports Parry's primrose, penstemon, and phlox, all set against vibrant green grass. Butterflies are abundant here as well.

Wildlife

America's national parks are known for their great vistas and fantastic rock formations, but they also preserve another treasure: wildlife.

Bison at Lamar Valley, Yellowstone National Park

In fact, national parks rank among the best places to see interesting and rare wildlife. Late summer marks a particularly good time for wildlife viewing at many parks as most mothers bring out their young by that time of the year.

Given the breadth of national park locations, there's also the opportunity to see almost every kind of North American wildlife, from those that live on mountains, in marine environments, and in the tropics to those that make their homes on prairies, deserts, and in temperate forests.

Mountains: Travelers can explore the "Serengeti of North America" on the Lamar Valley Trail at Wyoming's Yellowstone National Park. Like the mountain-ringed African plain, Lamar Valley serves as home to the classic megafauna that define North America. Bison, elk, grizzlies, black bears, wolves, coyotes, eagles, osprey and more all can be found at this high elevation. Coyotes also can be seen wandering about, looking for a meal while bald eagles and osprey grace the skies. Grizzlies reside in the hilly woods, but they and the area's other big two predators – black bears and wolf packs – prefer to remain under cover than be seen.

Marine: You can encounter an array of marine wildlife on the Beach Trail at Alaska's Glacier Bay National Park. Low tide also provides an opportunity to see intertidal life. As the waters retreat into the ocean – and water levels here can fall 25 vertical feet, among the greatest extremes in the world – a number of animals and plants are exposed. Don't be surprised to spot starfish and snails on the sands and grasses. On shore, a variety of sea birds gather and fly over, often nabbing exposed intertidal creatures for a meal. During those first moments of sunlight, watch for humpback whales, harbor porpoise, puffins, sea otters, and Steller sea lions, frolicking and feeding in the mouth of the bay. Bring binoculars. If lucky, you'll also hear the blow of humpback whales.

Tropics: Tropical wildlife can be safely seen from the Anhinga Trail at Florida's Everglades National Park. The trail's boardwalk takes you over open water where you can watch for alligators peeking out of a river, as well as turtles, herons and egrets. Winter marks the best season to see the most wildlife. A number of birds spend their time in the Everglades after migrating from a northern clime. Among those you can spot are the double breasted cormorant, great egret, great blue heron, snowy egret, tricolored heron, white ibis and woodstork. Turkey vultures congregate in the marsh during the early morning hours.

Prairies: North America's largest mammal – the bison – freely roams North Dakota's Theodore Roosevelt National Park, and the Buckhorn Trail is an excellent place to spot them and other Great Plains wildlife. The trail includes a prairie dog

Gila woodpecker, Saguaro National Park

town that stretches for about a mile. You'll be able to spot them barking from their burrow entrances as they keep an eye out for predators. Hawks, coyotes and rattlesnakes are among the creatures hoping to make an unsuspecting prairie dog its dinner.

Deserts: Four desert ecosystems can be found in North America, and the park closest to a major metro area offers among the best spots to see wildlife of these dry climes. Outside of Tucson, Ariz., Saguaro National Park's Douglas Spring Trail crosses the Rincon Mountain District (Saguaro Park East), providing the chance to see coyotes, roadrunners, jackrabbits, quail and Gila woodpeckers. All five of those creatures thrive in the Sonoran Desert, which stretches across Arizona and northern Mexico, as well as good portions of the continent's other three desert ecosystems.

Temperate forests: Great Smoky Mountains National Park, though stretching across the Appalachian Mountains, offers the opportunity to see many of the animals that reside in temperate forests covering much of the continent east of the Mississippi River. The Deep Creek/Indian Falls trails in the park's North Carolina section sports Eastern cottontail rabbit, groundhogs, river otter, and white-tailed deer. Also present but much more elusive, as they keep to themselves, are black bear, bobcat, coyote, red fox, red wolf, and wild boar.

Winter

Most travelers think of summer as the best time to hit national parks – but winter also offers several spectacular sights that make for memorable visits.

So when the snow starts falling, consider a road trip to one of the following parks.

Birders paradise: Winter marks the best time to hike Florida's Everglades National Park, as the subtropical climate means unbearably hot and buggy summers. Indeed, a number of birds already know this and spend their time in the Everglades after migrating from a northern clime. Among those you can spot on the Anhinga Trail are the double breasted cor-

Golden Canyon, Death Valley National Park

morant, great egret, great blue heron, snowy egret, tricolored heron, white ibis and woodstork; turkey vultures congregate during the early morning hours.

Wildlife sightings: Leafless trees and snow's white backdrop makes sighting large wildlife a lot easier in winter than summer. The Warner Point Nature Trail on the south rim of Colorado's Black Canyon of the Gunnison National Park offers the chance to spot elk and Rocky Mountain bighorn sheep. Look for the elk in clearings and the bighorn sheep on the rocky cliff sides.

Heavy waterfalls: At most parks, waterfalls are most active in spring and early summer, thanks to snow melts. Not so at Washington state's Olympic National Park. Rain is more likely there during winter, meaning the water flow is higher, making for a more spectacular creeks and falls. One good trail through the park's lush, old growth forest that ends at a waterfall is the Marymere Falls Trail.

Bearable heat: During summer, unbearable heats makes California's Death Valley National Park at best a pass through seen from a motor vehicle. The park's average high in January is a pleasant 67 degrees, though, making winter the perfect time to walk the foreboding desert landscape. Among those sights is the lowest point in North America. Badwater Basin sits 282 feet below sea level and can be accessed in a mile-long round trip hike.

Avoid the crowds: Visitation drops during winter at most parks, so the trade-off for bundling up in coat, cap and gloves is seeing the great scenery without all of the crowds. A good bet is Yosemite National Park's spectacular Yosemite Valley in California. The Lower Yosemite Fall Trail offers a number of fantastic views of Yosemite Falls in a 1.2-mile loop with the added coolness of falling water frozen in mid-flight on the granite rocks.

Christmas

A little secret: Among the best ways to escape holiday stress is a national park trip. Though often thought of as a summer destination, only a couple of the parks close in winter, and almost all offer warm, cozy and peaceful holiday experiences. A bonus is that almost all parks are less crowded during winter.

Here are five great holiday-themed must-do's at our national parks.

Winter wonderland, Yellowstone National Park: Book a getaway at the Old Faithful Snow Lodge, which can only be reached this time of year by snow coach or snowmobile. The Christmas-decorated lodge keeps its fireplace burning with plenty of hot cocoa for visitors. During the day, hike past "ghost

Christmas caroling in the cavern, Mammoth Cave National Park

trees," formed when the steam from the Old Faithful geyser freezes on pine tree needles. Bison with snow-covered manes often feed across the geyser valley.

Polar Express train ride, Cuyahoga Valley National Park: Each December prior to Christmas, the Cuyahoga Valley Scenic Railroad's Polar Express chugs through the scenic Ohio park. Among the highlights on the refurbished passenger train is a reading of the children's book "Polar Express," which inspired a movie and this trip. Many passengers ride the train in their pajamas! If in the Southwest, a private company also runs a Polar Express to Grand Canyon National Park.

Luminaria-lit skiing: Denali National Park: Every December, rangers light the small paper lanterns that line ski trails at the Alaska park. Visitors also can snowshoe or stroll the route, which leaves from the Murie Science and Learning

Center, Denali's Winter Visitor Center. Several other National Park Service sites offering luminaria displays and hikes including Florida's De Soto National Memorial and Arizona's Tonto National Monument.

Snowshoe wildlife hike, Rocky Mountain National Park: Ranger-led snowshoe tours lead visitors of this Colorado park to a variety of wildlife, including elk, coyotes, deer and snowshoe hares. The trail is utterly quiet as snow-capped mountains and evergreens rise around you on all sides.

Caroling in a cave, Mammoth Cave National Park: In early December, the Kentucky park holds Christmas carol singing in the world's longest cave system. It's a tradition that goes back to 1883 when local residents held the first Christmas celebration in the cave's passageways.

Historical sites

While the National Park Service's 59 major parks largely focus on protecting natural wonders and wilderness, they also preserve some historical sites. While many are merely ruins, others are in just as good of shape (if not better) than when they originally stood.

Historic Fort Jefferson: At Dry Tortugas National Park, you can visit a fort used during the Civil War. Built with more than 16 million bricks during the mid-1800s, Fort Jefferson is the Western Hemisphere's largest masonry structure. Six walls and towers with a moat make up the fort's outer area on Garden Key.

19th Century Mining Town: Crossing a thick rolling woodland, the Colorado River Trail at Rocky Mountain National Park offers nice views of Colorado River, arguably the Southwest's most important waterway. The trail to the ruins of an 19th century mining town, Lulu City, in a 6.2-miles round trip with 320-

John Oliver cabin in Cades Cove, Great Smoky Mountains National Park

foot elevation gain.

Appalachian life: A number of great day hikes allow visitors to explore the Great Smoky Mountain National Park's rich history. Pioneer cabins and mills await on several short day hikes, including those at Cades Code and Mingus Mill.

Butterfield Stage station: Along the Texas-New Mexico border, families can step back into the Old West and experience the remoteness of what once was a welcome sign to travelers: a Butterfield Stage station in the Guadalupe Mountains. The 0.75-mile round trip Pinery Trail marks a great day hike for families at Guadalupe National Park. The trail leads to the ruins of the Pinery Station, a once favored stop on the original 2,800-mile Butterfield Overland Mail Route.

Trees

Among the most fantastical sights at our national parks are

trees. Whether they be gigantic, fossilized, or older than the hills (figuratively speaking), they're certain to awe. Here are six great tree sites to visit.

Sequoias: Your family will feel like hobbits walking through scenes from "The Lord of the Rings" movies on the General Grant Tree Trail at Kings Canyon National Park. The 0.5-mile trail heads through the General Grant Grove of giant sequoias. More than 120 sequoias in the grove exceed 10 feet in diameter and most tower several stories over your head.

Redwoods: Hiking families can enjoy a trip into what feels like the forest primeval on a segment of the Damnation Creek Trail in Redwood National Park. For those with younger children, a 1.2-mile round trip through just the redwoods section of the trail makes for more than an incredible, inspiring walk.

Bristlecone pines: On several of Great Basin National Park's glacial moraines rise incredibly ancient bristlecone pines, many nearly 5,000 years old, meaning they began growing as the ancient Egyptians built the pyramids. The 2.8-mile round trip Bristlecone Pine Trail allows you to walk among a grove of the trees, which scientists say likely are the oldest living organisms on Earth.

Joshua trees: Day hikers can enjoy a walk through a large Joshua tree forest in the desert above the Palm Springs, Calif., area. A segment of the Boy Scout Trail at Joshua Tree National Park runs through a grove for a 2.4-mile round trip. Technically not a tree, the unusual Joshua tree is a member of the lily family.

Chestnut trees: Day hikers can head through what used to be a grove of majestic chestnut trees. The Cades Cove Nature Trail runs 1.4-miles round trip trail (from the parking lot) and sits in Cades Cove, an isolated mountain valley that is a popular destination thanks to many well-preserved structures from

Base of General Grant Tree, Kings Canyon National Park

pioneer days. A few seedlings of the great chestnut remain.

Petrified forest: Families can hike the remains of a woodlands dating from the dinosaurs' earliest days on the Great Logs Trail in Petrified Forest National Park. The fairly easy walk consists of two loops that combine for a 0.6-mile round trip. Because of the hot Arizona weather, spring and autumn mark the best time to hike the trail.

Learn more about these and many other great national park trails in the author's "Best Sights to See at America's National Parks."

About the Author

Rob Bignell is a long-time hiker, editor, and author of the popular "Best Sights to See," "Hikes with Tykes," "Headin' to the Cabin," and "Hittin' the Trail" guidebooks and several other titles. He and his son Kieran have been hiking together for the past decade. Rob has served as an infantryman in the Army National Guard and taught middle school students in New Mexico and Wisconsin. His newspaper work has won several national and state journalism awards, from editorial writing to sports reporting. In 2001, *The Prescott Journal*, which he served as managing editor of, was named Wisconsin's Weekly Newspaper of the Year. Rob and Kieran live in Wisconsin.

CHECK OUT THESE OTHER HIKING BOOKS BY ROB BIGNELL

"Best Sights to See" series:
• America's National Parks
• Great Smoky Mountain National Park
• Rocky Mountain National Park

"Hikes with Tykes" series:
• Hikes with Tykes: A Practical Guide to Day Hiking with Children
• Hikes with Tykes: Games and Activities

"Headin' to the Cabin" series:
• Day Hiking Trails of Northeast Minnesota
• Day Hiking Trails of Northwest Wisconsin

"Hittin' the Trail" series:
National parks
• Grand Canyon National Park (ebook only)
Minnesota
• Gooseberry Falls State Park
• Split Rock Lighthouse State Park
Minnesota/Wisconsin
• Interstate State Park
• St. Croix National Scenic Riverway
Wisconsin
• Barron County
• Bayfield County
• Burnett County (ebook only)

- Chippewa Valley (Eau Claire, Chippewa, Dunn, Pepin counties)
- Crex Meadows Wildlife Area (ebook only)
- Douglas County
- Polk County
- St. Croix County
- Sawyer County
- Washburn County

GET CONNECTED!

Follow the author to learn about other great trails and for useful hiking tips:
- Blog: *hikeswithtykes.blogspot.com*
- Facebook: *dld.bz/fBq2C*
- Google+: *dld.bz/fBq2s*
- LinkedIn: *linkedin.com/in/robbignell*
- Pinterest: *pinterest.com/rbignell41*
- Twitter: *twitter.com/dayhikingtrails*
- Website: *dayhikingtrails.wordpress.com*

If you enjoyed this book,
please take a few moments to write a review of it.

Thank you!

Made in the USA
Coppell, TX
24 June 2021

58005440R00072